First World War

and Army of Occupation

War Diary

France, Belgium and Germany

14 DIVISION
41 Infantry Brigade
King's Royal Rifle Corps
7th Battalion
18 May 1915 - 26 January 1918

WO95/1896/3

The Naval & Military Press Ltd
www.nmarchive.com
Published in association with The National Archives

Published by

The Naval & Military Press Ltd

Unit 10 Ridgewood Industrial Park,

Uckfield, East Sussex,

TN22 5QE England

Tel: +44 (0) 1825 749494

www.naval-military-press.com

www.nmarchive.com

This diary has been reprinted in facsimile from the original. Any imperfections are inevitably reproduced and the quality may fall short of modern type and cartographic standards.

Contents

Document type	Place/Title	Date From	Date To
Heading	1896/3		
Heading	14th Division 41st Infy Bde 7th Bn K.R.R.C. May 1915-Jan 1918		
Heading	14th Division 7th K.R.R. Corps Vol I 18-31.5.15 Jan 18		
War Diary	Aldershot	18/05/1915	19/05/1915
War Diary	Boulogne	19/05/1915	20/05/1915
War Diary	Wotton	20/05/1915	20/05/1915
War Diary	Millain	26/05/1915	26/05/1915
War Diary	Zuytpeene	27/05/1915	27/05/1915
War Diary	Fletre	28/05/1915	28/05/1915
War Diary	Onderdom	29/05/1915	29/05/1915
War Diary	Near Ypres	30/05/1915	31/05/1915
Miscellaneous	5th Division. G. 321	29/05/1915	29/05/1915
Miscellaneous	7 K R R		
Heading	14th Division 7th K. R. R. C. Vol II		
War Diary	Near Ypres	01/06/1915	02/06/1915
War Diary	Zevecoten & Near Ypres	03/06/1915	03/06/1915
War Diary	Dickebusch	05/06/1915	06/06/1915
War Diary	Gordon Farm	10/06/1915	11/06/1915
War Diary	Zevecoten	13/06/1915	13/06/1915
War Diary	Poperinghe	14/06/1915	14/06/1915
War Diary	Onderdom	15/06/1915	16/06/1915
War Diary	Near Ypres	17/06/1915	18/06/1915
War Diary	Onderdom	19/06/1915	19/06/1915
War Diary	Near Vlamertinghe	19/06/1915	25/06/1915
War Diary	Near Ypres	29/06/1915	30/06/1915
Heading	14th Division 7th Rifle Brigade Vol III 1-31-7-15		
War Diary	Hooge	01/07/1915	08/07/1915
War Diary	Poperinghe 2 M. West Of	09/07/1915	22/07/1915
War Diary	Hooge	23/07/1915	30/07/1915
War Diary	Vlamerting	30/07/1915	30/07/1915
War Diary	Zouave Wood	30/07/1915	31/07/1915
War Diary	Near Hazebrouck	31/07/1915	31/07/1915
Miscellaneous	Casualty Return		
Heading	14th Division 7th K. R. R. C. Vol III 17-2.8.15		
Heading	War Diary Of 7th (Service) Bn. Kings Royal Rifle Corps From 1st July 1915 To 2nd August 1915		
War Diary	Trenches Opposite Bellewarde Farm E. Of Ypres	01/07/1915	08/07/1915
War Diary	2 Miles W. Of Poperinghe	08/07/1915	23/07/1915
War Diary	Vlamertinghe	24/07/1915	29/07/1915
War Diary	Hooge	30/07/1915	30/07/1915
War Diary	1 Mile E. Of Poperinghe	31/07/1915	02/08/1915
Heading	14th Division 7th K. R. R. C. Vol IV From 1-31.8.15		
Heading	War Diary Of 7th (Service) Bn. Kings Royal Rifle Corps From 1st To 31st Aug 1915		
War Diary	1 Mile E. Of Poperinghe	01/08/1915	10/08/1915
War Diary	1 Mile S W Of Watou	11/08/1915	13/08/1915
War Diary	Trenches E. Of Ypres	14/08/1915	30/08/1915
War Diary	1/2 Mile E. Of Watou	31/08/1915	31/08/1915
Heading	14th Div 7th K. R. R. C. Vol 5		

Miscellaneous	7th (Service) Bn. Kings Royal Rifle Corps. War Diary From 1st September 1915 To 31st October 1915		
War Diary	1/2 Mile E Of Watou	01/09/1915	05/09/1915
War Diary	Kaaie Salient & Brielen Rd. Ypres	06/09/1915	13/09/1915
War Diary	Trenches E. Of Ypres	14/09/1915	21/09/1915
War Diary	1 Mile E. Of Poperinghe	22/09/1915	24/09/1915
War Diary	White Chateau	25/09/1915	30/09/1915
War Diary	White Chateau Henin Rd.	01/10/1915	06/10/1915
War Diary	Trenches H 14 To H 19	07/10/1915	13/10/1915
War Diary	Huts Near Vlamertinghe	14/10/1915	31/10/1915
Heading	14th Division 7th K.R.R.C. Vol. 6 Nov. 15		
Heading	War Diary Of 7th (Service) Bn King's Royal Rifle Corps From 1st Nov 1915 To 30th Nov 1915		
War Diary	Huts Near Vlamertinghe	01/11/1915	02/11/1915
War Diary	L Farm	03/11/1915	05/11/1915
War Diary	Ypres	06/11/1915	06/11/1915
War Diary	Canal Bank	09/11/1915	09/11/1915
War Diary	B Huts Vlamertinghe	10/11/1915	19/11/1915
War Diary	Trenches B 13-15 S 13-15	19/11/1915	19/11/1915
War Diary	Trenches B 13	21/11/1915	22/11/1915
War Diary	Canal Bank	23/11/1915	26/11/1915
War Diary	Trenches B 13 Etc	26/11/1915	30/11/1915
Miscellaneous	7th Bn K. R. Rifles		
Heading	War Diary Of The 7th (Service) Bn King's Royal Rifle Corps		
War Diary	A Huts Vlamertinghe	01/12/1915	04/12/1915
War Diary	Trenches B 13 Etc	04/12/1915	08/12/1915
War Diary	A Camp W Of Poperinghe	09/12/1915	12/12/1915
War Diary	Trenches B.13.etc	12/12/1915	16/12/1915
War Diary	B. Huts W. Of Poperinghe	17/12/1915	24/12/1915
War Diary	Glympose Cottage Trenches	31/12/1915	07/01/1916
Miscellaneous	December 1915 Average Weekly Strength Was 86th Other Ranks.		
Heading	7th K. R. R. C. Vol 8 41 Bde		
Heading	War Diary Of 7th Battalion King's Royal Rifle Corps		
War Diary	Glympose Cottage Trenches	08/01/1916	31/01/1916
Miscellaneous	January 1915 Average Weekly Strength Was Officers 25 Or 939	01/02/1916	01/02/1916
Heading	7th (Service) Battalion The King's Royal Rifle Corps. War Diary From 1st February 1916 To 29th February 1916		
War Diary	Poperinghe	01/02/1916	10/02/1916
War Diary	Briel	11/02/1916	20/02/1916
War Diary	Naours	21/02/1916	21/02/1916
War Diary	Doullens	24/02/1916	24/02/1916
War Diary	Sombrin	25/02/1916	28/02/1916
War Diary	Arras	29/02/1916	29/02/1916
Miscellaneous	7th (Service) Bn King's Royal Rifles.	00/02/1916	00/02/1916
Heading	7th (Service) Battalion The King's Royal Rifle Corps. War Diary From 1st March 1916 To 31st March 1916		
War Diary	Arras	01/03/1916	19/03/1916
War Diary	Simencourt	20/03/1916	20/03/1916
War Diary	Arras	25/03/1916	31/03/1916
Miscellaneous	7th Bn Kings Royal Rifles	01/04/1916	01/04/1916
Heading	7th (Service) Battalion The King's Royal Rifle Corps. War Diary From 1st April 1916 To 30th April 1916		

War Diary	Arras	01/04/1916	12/04/1916
War Diary	Wanquetin	13/04/1916	18/04/1916
War Diary	Arras	19/04/1916	30/04/1916
Miscellaneous	7th (Service) Bn. King's Royal Rifles.	00/04/1916	00/04/1916
Heading	7th (Service) Battalion The King's Royal Rifle Corps War Diary From 1st To 31st May 1916		
War Diary	Arras I Sector Left Trenches	01/05/1916	04/05/1916
War Diary	Wanquetin	06/05/1916	06/05/1916
War Diary	Savy	09/05/1916	09/05/1916
War Diary	Maroeuil	16/05/1916	24/05/1916
War Diary	Mt St Eloy	25/05/1916	29/05/1916
Heading	7th (Service) Battalion The King's Royal Rifle Corps May 1916	01/06/1916	01/06/1916
Miscellaneous	War Diary From O.C 7th Bn King's Royal Rifles		
Heading	War Diary Of The 7th (Service) Battalion King's Royal Rifle Corps From 1st June 1916 To 30th June 1916		
War Diary	Mt St Eloy	01/06/1916	01/06/1916
War Diary	La Targette	02/06/1916	08/06/1916
War Diary	A. C. Q.	09/06/1916	20/06/1916
War Diary	Roclincourt	20/06/1916	27/06/1916
War Diary	St Nicholas	28/06/1916	30/06/1916
Miscellaneous	7th (Service) Battalion King's Royal Rifle Corps June 1916	30/06/1916	30/06/1916
Heading	War Diary Of 7th Bn., King's Royal Rifle Corps. From: 1st July, 1916 To: 31st July, 1916 Volume 15		
War Diary	St Nicholas	01/07/1916	02/07/1916
War Diary	Roclincourt	03/07/1916	09/07/1916
War Diary	Duisans	10/07/1916	10/07/1916
War Diary	Roclincourt	15/07/1916	21/07/1916
War Diary	Arras	21/07/1916	25/07/1916
War Diary	Duisans	29/07/1916	31/07/1916
Miscellaneous	7th Bn. Kings Royal Rifle Corps	30/07/1916	30/07/1916
Heading	14th Division. 41st Infantry Brigade. 1/7th Battalion King's Royal Rifle Corps August 1916		
Miscellaneous	7th (Service) Bn. King's Royal Rifle Corps War Diary From 1st August 1916 To 31st August 1916 Volume 16		
Miscellaneous	7th (Service) Bn King Royal Rifle Corps Aug 1916	31/08/1916	31/08/1916
War Diary	Gesaincourt	01/08/1916	07/08/1916
War Diary	Dernancourt	08/08/1916	10/08/1916
War Diary	Reserve	11/08/1916	11/08/1916
War Diary	Support	12/08/1916	13/08/1916
War Diary	Reserve	14/08/1916	19/08/1916
War Diary	Pommiers	20/08/1916	24/08/1916
War Diary	Hop Alley	24/08/1916	31/08/1916
Heading	7th (Service) Battalion The King's Royal Rifle Corps War Diary From 1st To 30th September 1916 Volume 17		
War Diary	Mettigny	01/09/1916	10/09/1916
War Diary	Dernancourt	10/09/1916	10/09/1916
War Diary	Fricourt	11/09/1916	11/09/1916
War Diary	Montauban	12/09/1916	14/09/1916
War Diary	Front Line	15/09/1916	16/09/1916
War Diary	Dernancourt	17/09/1916	22/09/1916
War Diary	Lucheux	23/09/1916	26/09/1916
War Diary	Trenches F.2 Sector	27/09/1916	30/09/1916
Miscellaneous	7th (S) Bn King's Royal Rifle Corps Sept 1916	30/09/1916	30/09/1916

Heading	7th (Service) Battalion The King's Royal Rifle Corps War Diary From 1st To 31st October 1916 Volume 18		
War Diary	F.2 Sector	02/10/1916	12/10/1916
War Diary	Riviere	15/10/1916	19/10/1916
War Diary	F.3 Sector	21/10/1916	23/10/1916
War Diary	Beaumetz	25/10/1916	25/10/1916
War Diary	Sombrin	26/10/1916	31/10/1916
Miscellaneous	7th (Service) Bn King's Royal Rifles October 1916	31/10/1916	31/10/1916
Heading	7th (Service) Battalion The King's Royal Rifle Corps War Diary From 1st To 30th November 1916 Volume 19		
War Diary	Sombrin	01/11/1916	30/11/1916
Miscellaneous	7th (S) Bn King's Royal Rifles November 1916	30/11/1916	30/11/1916
Heading	7th (Service) Battalion The King's Royal Rifle Corps War Diary From 1st December 1916 To 31st December 1916 Volume 20		
War Diary	Sombrin	01/12/1916	15/12/1916
War Diary	Beaumetz	17/12/1916	17/12/1916
War Diary	F 1 Sector	22/12/1916	24/12/1916
War Diary	Riviere	28/12/1916	28/12/1916
Miscellaneous	7th (Service) Bn King's Royal Rifles December 1916	31/12/1916	31/12/1916
Heading	7th (Service) Bn King's Royal Rifle Corps War Diary From 1st To 31st January 1917 Volume 21		
War Diary	Riviere	01/01/1917	02/01/1917
War Diary	F Sector	03/01/1917	09/01/1917
War Diary	Beaumetz	10/01/1917	11/01/1917
War Diary	Simencourt	12/01/1917	15/01/1917
War Diary	F Sector	16/01/1917	21/01/1917
War Diary	Riviere	22/01/1917	27/01/1917
War Diary	F Sector	28/01/1917	31/01/1917
Miscellaneous	7th (S) Bn King's Royal Rifle Corps January 1917	31/01/1917	31/01/1917
Heading	7th (Service) Battalion The King's Royal Rifle Corps War Diary From 1st To 28th February 1917 Volume 22		
War Diary	F2 Sector	01/02/1917	02/02/1917
War Diary	Simencourt	02/02/1917	03/02/1917
War Diary	Sombrin	04/02/1917	26/02/1917
Miscellaneous	7th (S) Bn King's Royal Rifles February 1917	28/02/1917	28/02/1917
Heading	7th (Service) Battalion. The King's Royal Rifle Corps War Diary From 1st To 31st March 1917 Volume 23		
War Diary	Sombrin	01/03/1917	15/03/1917
War Diary	St Moncourt	16/03/1917	21/03/1917
War Diary	Arras	22/03/1917	23/03/1917
War Diary	Bluff Cave	24/03/1917	31/03/1917
Miscellaneous	7th (S) Bn King's Royal Rifle Corps March 1917	31/03/1917	31/03/1917
Heading	7th (Service) Battalion. The King's Royal Rifle Corps War Diary From 1st To 30th April 1917 Volume 24		
War Diary	Ronville Caves	01/04/1917	03/04/1917
War Diary	Dainville	05/04/1917	12/04/1917
Miscellaneous	A Form. Messages And Signals.		
Miscellaneous	7th (S) Bn K. R. R. C.	29/04/1917	29/04/1917
Miscellaneous	41st Inf. Bde	30/04/1917	30/04/1917
Miscellaneous	A Form. Messages And Signals.		
Miscellaneous	D.A. 56/10	07/04/1917	07/04/1917
Miscellaneous	Tank Routes		
Operation(al) Order(s)	41st Infantry Brigade Operation Order No. 131	07/04/1917	07/04/1917

Heading	War Diary Of 7th (Service) Bn. King's Royal Rifle Corps. From 26th April 1917 To 31st May 1917 (Volume 25)		
War Diary	In Support	26/04/1917	28/04/1917
War Diary	In The Line	28/04/1917	01/05/1917
War Diary	In Support	01/05/1917	03/05/1917
War Diary	In The Line	04/05/1917	04/05/1917
War Diary	In Support	05/05/1917	13/05/1917
War Diary	In The Line	14/05/1917	24/05/1917
War Diary	Bearvains	25/05/1917	31/05/1917
Miscellaneous	7th (Service) Bn King's Royal Rifles.	31/05/1917	31/05/1917
Heading	7th (Service) Battalion The King's Royal Rifle Corps War Diary From 26-5-1917 To 30-6-1917 Volume 26		
Miscellaneous	41st Inf. Bde.	30/06/1917	30/06/1917
Heading	Cover For Documents. Vol. 28 7th Bn. K.R.R.C. 1-6-17 To 30.6.17		
War Diary	Beaurains	26/05/1917	01/06/1917
War Diary	Nepal Trench	02/06/1917	09/06/1917
War Diary	Beaurains	10/06/1917	11/06/1917
War Diary	Monchiet	12/06/1917	12/06/1917
War Diary	Saulty	13/06/1917	13/06/1917
War Diary	Louvencourt	14/06/1917	30/06/1917
War Diary	Beaurains	26/05/1917	01/06/1917
War Diary	Nepal Trench	02/06/1917	09/06/1917
War Diary	Beaurains	10/06/1917	11/06/1917
War Diary	Manchiet	12/06/1917	12/06/1917
War Diary	Saulty	13/06/1917	13/06/1917
War Diary	Louvencourt	14/06/1917	30/06/1917
Miscellaneous	7th (S) Bn King's Royal Rifle Corps	30/06/1917	30/06/1917
Heading	7th (Service) Battalion. The King's Royal Rifle Corps War Diary From 1st To 31st July 1917 Volume 27		
War Diary	France In The Field	01/07/1917	30/07/1917
Miscellaneous	7th (S) Bn King's Royal Rifles.	31/07/1917	31/07/1917
Heading	7th (Service) Battalion The King's Royal Rifle Corps War Diary From 1st To 31st August 1917 Volume 28		
War Diary		01/08/1917	06/08/1917
War Diary	Hondeghem	07/08/1917	15/08/1917
War Diary	Dickebusch	15/08/1917	15/08/1917
War Diary	Trenches	16/08/1917	17/08/1917
War Diary	Dickebusch	20/08/1917	20/08/1917
War Diary	Chateau Segard	22/08/1917	22/08/1917
War Diary	Dickebusch	23/08/1917	23/08/1917
War Diary	Trenches	24/08/1917	27/08/1917
War Diary	Dickebusch Meteren	28/08/1917	28/08/1917
Miscellaneous	7th (S) Bn. Kings Royal Rifles	31/08/1917	31/08/1917
Heading	War Diary Of 7th (Service) Battalion The King's Royal Rifle Corps From 1st Sep. To 30th Sep. 1917 Volume 29		
War Diary	Meteren	01/09/1917	01/09/1917
War Diary	Waterloo Camp	02/09/1917	02/09/1917
War Diary	Neuve Eglise	05/09/1917	05/09/1917
War Diary	Messines	12/09/1917	12/09/1917
War Diary	Front Line	16/09/1917	16/09/1917
War Diary	Neuve Eglise	20/09/1917	29/09/1917
Miscellaneous	7th (S) Bn Kings Royal Rifle Corps	30/09/1917	30/09/1917

Heading	War Diary Of 7th (S) Bn., King's Royal Rifle Corps. From 1st October, 1917 To 31st October, 1917 Volume XXX		
War Diary	Neuve Eglise	01/10/1917	01/10/1917
War Diary	Reninghelst	06/10/1917	06/10/1917
War Diary	Dickebusch	09/10/1917	09/10/1917
War Diary	Trenches	10/10/1917	10/10/1917
War Diary	Ridgewood	16/10/1917	18/10/1917
War Diary	Bedford House	19/10/1917	19/10/1917
War Diary	La Clytte	22/10/1917	22/10/1917
War Diary	Meteren	23/10/1917	23/10/1917
Miscellaneous	7th (S) Bn Kings Royal Rifles	31/10/1917	31/10/1917
Heading	War Diary Of 7th (Service) Bn. The King's Royal Rifle Corps From 1st To 30th November 1917 Volume 31		
War Diary	Meteren	01/11/1917	01/11/1917
War Diary	Longuenesse	11/11/1917	29/11/1917
War Diary	Vlamertinghe	30/11/1917	30/11/1917
Miscellaneous	7th (S) Bn Kings Royal Rifle Corps	30/11/1917	30/11/1917
Heading	War Diary Of The 7th (Service) Battn The King's Royal Rifle Corps Volume 32 From 1st To 31st Dec 1917		
War Diary	Vlamertinghe	01/12/1917	01/12/1917
War Diary	California Camp	02/12/1917	02/12/1917
War Diary	Trenches	05/12/1917	05/12/1917
War Diary	Brandhoek	08/12/1917	08/12/1917
War Diary	Junction Camp	19/12/1917	19/12/1917
War Diary	Trenches	22/12/1917	22/12/1917
War Diary	Wieltje	26/12/1917	26/12/1917
War Diary	Leuline	27/12/1917	27/12/1917
Miscellaneous	7th (S) Bn. K. R. R. Corps	31/12/1917	31/12/1917
Heading	7th (Service) Battalion The King's Royal Rifle Corps War Diary From 1st To 31st January 1918 Volume 33		
War Diary	Leuline	31/12/1917	02/01/1918
War Diary	Vaux-Sur-Somme	03/01/1918	26/01/1918
Miscellaneous	7th (S) Bn King's Royal Rifle Corps	31/01/1918	31/01/1918
Miscellaneous	7th (S) Bn. King's Royal Rifle Corps		
Miscellaneous	7th (Service) Bn. King's Royal Rifle Corps		
Miscellaneous	A Coy 7th K. R. Rifles		
Miscellaneous	B Coy 7th K R R		
Miscellaneous	1st "C" Coy 7th K. R. R. C.		
Miscellaneous	2 "C" Coy 7th K. R. R. C.		
Miscellaneous	3 "C" Coy 7th K. R. R. C.		
Miscellaneous	4 "C" Coy 7th K. R. R. C.		
Miscellaneous	5 "C" Coy 7th K. R. R. C.		
Miscellaneous	6 "C" Coy 7th K. R. R. C.		
Miscellaneous	7 "C" Coy 7th K. R. R. C.		
Miscellaneous	8 "C" Coy 7th K. R. R. C.		
Miscellaneous	D Coy 7th K R Rifles		

14TH DIVISION

41ST INFY BDE

7TH BN K.R.R.C.

MAY 1915-JAN 1918

Page I

Instructions regarding War Diaries and Intelligence Summaries are contained in F. S. Regs., Part II. and the Staff Manual respectively. Title pages will be prepared in manuscript.

WAR DIARY
or
~~INTELLIGENCE SUMMARY.~~

(*Erase heading not required.*)

Army Form C. 2118.

Place	Date	Hour	Summary of Events and Information	Remarks and references to Appendices
~~[illegible]~~ Aldershot	18/5/15	6.30am	Regimental Transport left Aldershot for Southampton + Havre -	
Aldershot	19/5/15	3.40pm	Battalion left Aldershot for Folkestone + Boulogne -	
Boulogne	19/5/15	11.15pm	Battalion arrived Boulogne + spent night in rest camp -	
Boulogne	20/5/15	9.30pm	Battalion left Boulogne by train for WOTTON	
Wotton	20/5/15	12.30pm	Battalion arrived Wotton and billeted at MILLAIN until May 26th	
Millain	26/5/15	8.30am	Battalion marched to ZUYTPEENE and billeted there	
ZUYTPEENE	27/5/15	6.50am	Battalion marched to FLÈTRE + billeted there	
~~OUDERDOM~~ FLETRE	28/5/15	8. am	Battalion marched to OUDERDOM + billeted there in huts -	
OUDERDOM	29/5/15		Battalion commenced eight days course of instruction in Trench warfare - attached to the 14th Inf Bde - into whose trenches they went under the instruction of the D.C.L.I. - the E. Surrey Regt - the Devon Regt + the Manchester Regt - near YPRES -	
Near YPRES	30/5/15		Battalion lost 5 men wounded whilst trench digging -	
Near YPRES	31/5/15		Battalion lost 1 man killed + 1 wounded in trenches and 2 men wounded trench digging -	

[illegible] Capt + Adjt
K.R.Rifles

1577 Wt. W10791/1773 500,000 1/15 D. D. & L. A.D.S.S./Forms/C. 2118.

5th Division.
G.321.

1. 7th Bn. K.R.R. will find a working party of 350 with proper complement of Officers, to work on the ZILLEBEKE switch to-night. The party to be found from the two companies not going into trenches.

All battalion tools will be taken, and the deficit made up at the KRUISSTRAAT R.E. Depot at road junction H.24.a. 4/8.

No tools should therefore be taken with the two companies going into the trenches.

2. The party should march so as to reach the KRUISSTRAAT R.E. Depot at 8.15 p.m. On completion of work they will rejoin the remainder of the two companies in the dug-outs at H.23.a. 8/8.

3. Guides for the party from KRUISSTRAAT R.E. Depot will be provided by 59th Field Co. R.E. and will be in waiting at Headquarters of 59th Co. R.E. (house on north side of road H.23.b. 6/8).

4. An Officer and two N.C.O's. of the party will be at Headquarters 59th Co. R.E. by 5 p.m; an Officer 59th Co. will then take them on by daylight to show them the work which the party is to carry out.

5. Acknowledge by wire.

5th Division, Lt.Colonel,

29th May, 1915. General Staff, 5th Division.

Copies to -

C.R.E.
59th Co. R.E.
7th Bn. K.R.R..

14th Division

121/5931

7th K.R.R.C.

Vol: II

Instructions regarding War Diaries and Intelligence Summaries are contained in F. S. Regs., Part II. and the Staff Manual respectively. Title pages will be prepared in manuscript.

WAR DIARY
or
INTELLIGENCE SUMMARY.
(Erase heading not required.)

Army Form C. 2118.

Place	Date	Hour	Summary of Events and Information	Remarks and references to Appendices
Near Ypres	1/6/15		Battalion under instruction in trenches of 14th Infantry Brigade -	
Near Ypres	2/6/15		Battalion under instruction in trenches of 14th Infantry Brigade -	
Zevecoten + Near Ypres	3/6/15		C + D Coys moved to Huts at Zevecoten - A + B Coys under instruction in trenches 14th Inf Brigade -	
Dickebusch	5/6/15		Battalion moved to Canada Huts -	
Dickebusch	6/6/15		Battalion moved to Pioneer Farm as Reserve battalion to Brigade in trenches P_2 to O5 -	
Gordon Farm	10/6/15		Battalion took over trenches P_2 to O5	
Gordon Farm	11/6/15		Captain E. Fairlie wounded -	
Zevecoten	13/6/15		Battalion relieved from trenches by Monmouthshire Rgt and moved to huts E. of Zevecoten -	
Poperinghe	14/6/15		Marched to Bivouacs W. of Poperinghe -	
Ouderdom	15/6/15		Battalion marched to huts at Ouderdom and became reserve to 5th Corps	
Ouderdom	16/6/15	2.50am	Attack against Bellewaarde Farm commenced by 5th Corps -	
		11.30am	Battalion moved up to trenches in reserve S. of Ypres -	
Near Ypres	17/6/15		In trenches S. of Ypres in reserve to 5th Corps -	
Near Ypres	18/6/15	8.30pm	Battalion moved to Ouderdom -	

Instructions regarding War Diaries and Intelligence Summaries are contained in F. S. Regs., Part II. and the Staff Manual respectively. Title pages will be prepared in manuscript.

WAR DIARY
or
~~INTELLIGENCE SUMMARY.~~
(Erase heading not required.)

Army Form C. 2118.

Place	Date	Hour	Summary of Events and Information	Remarks and references to Appendices
Ouderdom	19/6/15		In huts at Ouderdom	
near Vlamertinghe	20/6/15		Battalion moved to B. Huts	
near Vlamertinghe	21/6/15		Battalion shelled in B. Huts during afternoon - no casualties	
"	22/6/15		Battalion shelled in B. Huts during afternoon - no casualties	
"	23/6/15		Battalion shelled in B. Huts during afternoon - no casualties	
"	24/6/15		Battalion shelled in B. Huts during morning - afternoon and night - no casualties - Transport moved back 1 mile towards Poperinghe -	
"	25/6/15		Battalion in B. Huts -	
Near Ypres	29/6/15	[illegible] pm	Battalion took over trenches from 63rd Inf Bde -	
"	30/6/15		Battalion in trenches - C + D Coys in firing trench - B Coy in support A Coy in Reserve - 2Lt R. H. Somers - Smith killed - Casualties 1 officer killed 1/Lt R. Boothroyd - wounded 1 officer wounded other Ranks - 4 killed 6 wounded	

A H Lewis (?) Capt & Adjt
7 K.R.R.

1577 Wt. W10791/1773 500,000 1/15 D. D. & L. A.D.S.S./Forms/C 2118.

41/14th Division

121/6357

7th Rifle Brigade

Vol: III

Jul 1 - 31-7-15

Army Form C. 2118.

(10)

Instructions regarding War Diaries and Intelligence Summaries are contained in F. S. Regs., Part II. and the Staff Manual respectively. Title pages will be prepared in manuscript.

WAR DIARY
or
~~INTELLIGENCE~~ SUMMARY.

(Erase heading not required.)

1915. Hour, Date, Place	Summary of Events and Information	Remarks and references to Appendices
HOOGE. 1 July	Still in trenches.	
	~~No 3365 No 252 Rifn PARKER~~ [initials]	
	No 298 Rifn WALLIS A Coy. Wounded	
	No 10 Cpl WANSBROUGH A Coy "	
	D Coy had 2 gas shells in their Trenches, no casualties, parapet much damaged and gas remained for about 18 hrs in spite of spraying.	
	Very little wind. [initials]	
" 2 July.	Still in Trenches.	
	No 3365 Rifn LAWTON A Coy Killed.	Buried in Trench [illegible] I 12 c 4.4
	No 5079 " L. VEDOVA A Coy Killed.	
	No 2232 A/Cpl MILES C Coy. Killed.	Buried at Ecole de Bienfaisance East of YPRES.
	No 7249 Rifn BURROUGHS D Coy Wounded	
	No 1762 " SPRINGETT C Coy "	
	No 554 " IZARD B Coy "	
	No 1454 " HULSE B Coy "	
	No 1379 " BURGESS B Coy "	
	No 2908 " OLDFIELD C Coy } Suffering from effects of a gas shell.	
	No 7510 " GOLDNEY C "	
	No 798 " MARRIOTT C "	
	No 3033 " WROE C "	[initials]

Army Form C. 2118. (11)

Instructions regarding War Diaries and Intelligence Summaries are contained in F. S. Regs., Part II. and the Staff Manual respectively. Title pages will be prepared in manuscript.

WAR DIARY
or
~~INTELLIGENCE SUMMARY.~~
(Erase heading not required.)

1915. Hour, Date, Place		Summary of Events and Information	Remarks and references to Appendices
HOOGE.	3 July	Still in trenches. No alteration in distribution of Companies. Rations are carried from dumping ground to Companies and Bn. Hd. Qrs. by D. Coy. No Casualties. [initials]	
"	4 July.	(SUNDAY) No 6056 Rfn. FRENCH. A Coy. wounded. Considering amount of shelling which took place today this is extraordinary. [initials]	
"	5 July.	No 5084 Rfn. WHITTALL. A Coy. wounded No 1360 " POSTLETHWAITE. B Coy " No 11800 " STURROCK. A Coy " No 11776 " STONE. A Coy. " accident. No 2206 " DRAKE. C " Slightly (at duty) No 6054 " MARSHALL. A " wounded No 5078 " VEDOVA. E. A Coy " No 3034 " BIGGS C " " No 7396 " NAPIER. B " " No 5083 A/Cpl RICE A " " A normal day in trenches as regards activity. [initials]	

(73989) W4141—463. 400,000. 9/14. H.&J.Ltd. Forms/C. 2118/10.

Instructions regarding War Diaries and Intelligence Summaries are contained in F. S. Regs., Part II. and the Staff Manual respectively. Title pages will be prepared in manuscript.

WAR DIARY
or
~~INTELLIGENCE SUMMARY.~~

(Erase heading not required.)

Army Form C. 2118.

Hour, Date, Place	Summary of Events and Information	Remarks and references to Appendices
HOOGE. 6 July. 5.30 am	Batt. under arms during an attack N. of YPRES. Our guns bombarded enemy opposite us in order to mislead enemy as to locality of attack. We were heavily bombarded in reply. After 9 a.m. things were suspiciously quiet until 4 pm when shelling our supports and communication trenches received with more activity than usual.	
	No 511 Rfn BIRSE. A Coy. Killed.	Buried [illegible] I. 12. [illegible]
	No 82 " WYATT " " Wounded	
	No 263 " RIFFELL "	
	No 11777 " TUCKER "	
	No 397 " TOBIAS "	
" 7 July.	No 11733 " LINFIELD A Coy Killed.	Buried. I. [illegible]
	439 " WELLS. A " ~~wounded~~ Killed.	
	No 3226 " DANIELS D wounded, splinter whilst laying wire.	
	" Died at dressing Station on 9th inst.	Buried. [illegible]
"	No 2274 " J. HARDEN. C " Killed on 5th inst whilst attached to 8th Bn R.B. Machine Gun.	Buried. I. [illegible]

(73989) W4141—463. 400,000. 9/14. H.&J.Ltd. Forms/C. 2118/10.

Army Form C. 2118. (13)

Instructions regarding War Diaries and Intelligence Summaries are contained in F. S. Regs., Part II. and the Staff Manual respectively. Title pages will be prepared in manuscript.

WAR DIARY
or
INTELLIGENCE SUMMARY.
(*Erase heading not required.*)

Hour, Date, Place	Summary of Events and Information	Remarks and references to Appendices
HOOGE. 8th July	No 497 Rfn THOMAS. A. Coy. wounded	
	427 " BROWN " " "	
	3200 Sgt. H.G. CUTLER A. Coy "	
	338 Rfn APLIN A. Coy "	
	5077 " HADKINSON " "	
midnight.	Relieved in trenches by 9th Bn Rifle Brigade	[illegible]
POPERINGHE. 2 M. west of. 9th July 7 a.m.	Arrived and bivouacked for rest.	[illegible]
" 10th July	Resting	
" 11th "	Sunday. 7 p.m 1 off and 50 men started to work East of YPRES digging in telephone wire.	[illegible]
" 12th "	Resting. 1 off + 50 men ditto.	[illegible]
" 13th "	Hot baths for Battalion. 1 off + 50 men do. do.	[illegible]
" 14th "	Nothing	[illegible]
" 15th "	1 off + 50 men do. do.	[illegible]

Army Form C. 2118. (14)

Instructions regarding War Diaries and Intelligence Summaries are contained in F. S. Regs., Part II. and the Staff Manual respectively. Title pages will be prepared in manuscript.

WAR DIARY
or
~~INTELLIGENCE SUMMARY~~.
(Erase heading not required.)

Hour, Date, Place		Summary of Events and Information	Remarks and references to Appendices
POPERINGHE. 2 M. West of	July 16th 7 pm	4 offs + 300 men digging at front at night.	[initials]
	17th "	" " " " " No 7145 Rfn A. E. KRAMER. C Coy wounded.	[initials]
	18th "	SUNDAY. 2 offs + 100 men " " "	[initials]
	19th "	offs & 200 men at work afternoon at H.O.4.b.	[initials]
	20th "	C.O. + Coy Commrs to HOOGE with a view to taking over trenches in I 18. tomorrow. Relief postponed 24 hrs as we exploded a mine last night under HOOGE and the situation was not fit to relieve yet.	[initials]
	21st "	Draft 2 N.C.Os and 33 Rfn.	[initials]
	22nd " 10 a.m	D Coy and bombers left to relieve portion of trenches by daylight. Remainder relieving at night. Relieved 1st Bn Gordon Highlanders. C + D in front. A + B in reserve. [initials]	Fighting strength 22 July Officers R + F

(15)

Instructions regarding War Diaries and Intelligence Summaries are contained in F. S. Regs., Part II. and the Staff Manual respectively. Title pages will be prepared in manuscript.

WAR DIARY

or

~~INTELLIGENCE SUMMARY.~~

(Erase heading not required.)

Army Form C. 2118.

Hour, Date, Place			Summary of Events and Information		Remarks and references to Appendices	
HOOGE.	July 23 –	1 a.m.	Relief completed.			
		8 a.m.	Several casualties from Trench Mortars about Crater		Casualties. APPENDIX	~~A~~.
		3 p.m.	Bombing duel at Barrier W of Crater. 1 officer wounded.	[initials]		
	July 24 –	8 a.m.	A small mine exploded by Germans left of crater, barrier destroyed and trench cratered. Succeeded in rebuilding barrier.	[initials]	" "	~~B~~
		9.30 p.m.	S.O.S message from Crater. It appears that the Germans have built a new trench 15 yds beyond crater, and started a bomb attack on the trench we captured. Our Guns opened very quickly and we responded also with bombs, the attack ceased	[initials]	" "	~~C~~
	July 25	2 p.m.	Mortars again active – no casualties from them.			
		7 p.m.	German Aeroplane set on fire by one of ours, it fell near ZOUAVE WOOD – 3 occupants – Killed	[initials]	" "	~~C~~
	July 26th	"	Relieved C + D by A + B respectively. Nothing unusual to report. Draft of 50 arrived at Battalion and distributed to Companies. Lts Pope – Fraser – + Purdon reported for duty.	[initials]	Lt E. W. Pope, S. F. Purdon, W. N. Fraser } Joined Battn "	~~D~~
	July 27th	"	Relieved B Coy by D Coy. A Coy were quite ready to remain till end of tour.	[initials]	" "	~~E~~
	July 28	"	Nothing unusual. Shelled by own Artillery.	[initials]	" "	~~F~~

(73989) W4141—463. 400,000. 9/14. H.&J.Ltd. Forms/C. 2118/10.

Instructions regarding War Diaries and Intelligence Summaries are contained in F. S. Regs., Part II. and the Staff Manual respectively. Title pages will be prepared in manuscript.

WAR DIARY

or

~~INTELLIGENCE~~ ~~SUMMARY.~~

(Erase heading not required.)

Army Form C. 2118.

Place	Date	Hour	Summary of Events and Information	Remarks and references to Appendices
HOOGE.	July 29th	11.50pm	Relieved by 8th Bn Rifle Bde.	
	July 30th	1.20am	Relief completed.	
VLAMERTING[HE]	"	3.45am	Battalion arrived at [illegible] Camp	
		4.45	Received orders to be prepared to return to YPRES in support.	
		5.30am	Orders received to return YPRES with as much S.A.A. as possible.	
		7am	Having filled water bottles and issued rations and extra S.A.A. the Battalion started and halted on the road between [illegible] and KRUISSTRAAT till 11.30am. The C.O. and Adjt having in the meantime been to 41st Bde H.Q. [illegible] YPRES [illegible]. Heard that HOOGE had been captured by the enemy. Ordered to march via ZILLEBEKE to ZOUAVE WOOD and to form up in [illegible] of [illegible] for counter attack.	
			The communication trench was very muddy and bad, the head of the Batt. in single file reached ZOUAVE WOOD about 1.40 pm.	
ZOUAVE WOOD		[illegible] pm		
		2 pm	Bombardment by our artillery commenced for 3/4 hr. During this time the Battalion formed up in the wood in rear of 8th R.B. as follows —	

(73989) W4141—463. 400,000. 9/14. H.&J.Ltd. Forms/C. 2118/10.

Instructions regarding War Diaries and Intelligence Summaries are contained in F. S. Regs., Part II. and the Staff Manual respectively. Title pages will be prepared in manuscript.

WAR DIARY
or
~~INTELLIGENCE~~ SUMMARY.
(Erase heading not required.)

Army Form C. 2118. (17)

Hour, Date, Place	Summary of Events and Information	Remarks and references to Appendices
ZOUAVE WOOD. 30/July. 2 pm	C Coy in Column of Platoons on left of Communication trench called OLD BOND STREET B in similar formation on Right of C Trench A behind C in similar formation D behind B " " " with intervals between platoons of about 50 yds. All this time the Germans poured a terrific fire of heavy high explosive into the N Portion of the wood, making our preparation very difficult and causing many casualties.	
2.45 pm	Bombardment ceased and assault commenced. By request of O.C. 8th Bn our leading line started in support at once. Their exit from the wood was impeded by our barbed wire and owing to M.G. fire of the enemy very few got beyond the edge of the wood. From my Battn Hd Qrs where the Southern arm leaves the main wood I could observe and saw that the attack was not progressing as I could see none of our men outside the wood towards the objective. The flow of lines continued but none got beyond the wire. I reported that more men	

(73989) W4141—463. 400,000. 9/14. H.&J.Ltd. Forms/C. 2118/10.

Army Form C. 2118.

Instructions regarding War Diaries and Intelligence Summaries are contained in F. S. Regs., Part II. and the Staff Manual respectively. Title pages will be prepared in manuscript.

WAR DIARY
or
INTELLIGENCE SUMMARY.

(Erase heading not required.)

Hour, Date, Place	Summary of Events and Information	Remarks and references to Appendices

(73989) W4141—463. 400,000. 9/14. H.&J.Ltd. Forms/C. 2118/10.

Instructions regarding War Diaries and Intelligence Summaries are contained in F. S. Regs., Part II. and the Staff Manual respectively. Title pages will be prepared in manuscript.

WAR DIARY
or
INTELLIGENCE SUMMARY.
(Erase heading not required.)

Army Form C. 2118. (19)

Hour, Date, Place	Summary of Events and Information	Remarks and references to Appendices
near HAZEBROUCK. 31 July.	A correct casualty list is very hard to prepare without details from the Clearing Stations and owing to many being Killed and wounded beyond reach at present – the following is approximate – officers	
	Capt S.H. DRUMMOND Comm'g C Coy missing	
	Capt P. COLLINS 2nd in C. C " Killed	
	Lt G.W.L. TALBOT C " missing believed Killed	body since found. Killed
	2Lt G.F.O. DEVITT C " Killed (died of wounds the same evening)	
	Capt Hon C.D. FINCH. Comm'g B " wounded	
	2Lt F.E. MARRIOTT B. Killed	
	2Lt R.H. LAWSON B. wounded	
	Capt A.H. MILWARD Comm'g A. wounded	
	Capt F.B.H. DRUMMOND 2nd i/c A. wounded (lost arm)	
	Lt J.H. FOSDICK A. died of wounds on 31st.	
	Capt W.R. McILWAINE Comm'g D. Shock from explosion of bomb store.	
	2Lt A. GODSAL. Bn M.G. officer Killed.	
	During the week the Battalion has lost 8 officers Killed – 1 missing – 7 wounded all the Captains & 2nd in Commands of Coys are amongst these. Casualties in other ranks cannot be computed yet. Roughly 300 on July 30th	Fighting strength 1 Aug 14 Offs. 559 O.R.

[initials]

CASUALTY RETURN

24 hours ending

REGTL Nº	RANK + NAME			COY	KILLED	WOUNDED	SLIGHTLY WOUNDED AT DUTY	GASSED		EVACUATED	REMARKS
3445	Rfn	Kelly	E A	C		23.7.15					[illegible]
2843	"	Inman	E H	D		"					
1453	"	Bullock	W	HQ		"					
3105	"	Jackson	F	D		"					
7436	"	Emmett	F	"		"					
5067	"	Hitchcock	W	"			23.7.15				
1897	"	Eaton	T	"			"				
	2nd Lt	Shoveller	S H	C		23.7.15					
	"	Bert	T S	B	24.7.15						[illegible]
3449	Sgt	Hanson	R A	C	"						
2763	Rfn	Bird	H	"			24.7.15				
2360	"	Rogers	A G	B		24.7.15					
1375	"	Williams	W	"		"					
2066	"	Lloyd	J	C		"					
2493	"	Flack	J	D		"					

CASUALTY RETURN 24 hours ending

REGTL. Nº	RANK & NAME	COY.	KILLED	WOUNDED	SLIGHTLY WOUNDED AT DUTY	GASSED	MISSING	EVACUATED	REMARK Where buried
~~Capt~~	~~R W Hardy~~	~~D~~							
	Lt Merriam L P B	C		22-7-15					
20514	Rfn Palmer W	"		"					
6127	" Summer P	D		"					
	Capt Hardy R W	"	23-7-15						Crater Hooge
4980	Sgt Goodwin J A	"	"						"
1914	Rfn Gilbert A	"	"						"
7357	" Stilton A	"	"						"
6513	Cpl Summer J	C	"						Field nr [illegible]
3451	A/c Watson R T	"	"						"
8525	Rfn Fradman J	"	"						"
3203	" Skinner W	D	"						Crater Hooge
6063	" Gibbs W	"	"				23/7/15		"
7243	" Drury J L	"					"		
1974	" Banner B	"		23-7-15					
2512	Cpl Hands A	"		"					

CASUALTY RETURN 24 hours ending

REGT L No.	RANK & NAME			COY	KILLED	WOUNDED	SLIGHTLY WOUNDED AT DUTY	GASSED		EVACUATED	REMARKS
3393	Rfn	Brookes	A J	D		23-7-15					
3204	"	Lewell	C	"		"					
2351	"	White	H	"		"					
1591	"	Haycock	C W	"		"					
156	Sgt	Marks	G	"		"					
2688	Rfn	Wakefield	T	"		"					
527	"	Jenner	B	"		"					
6121	"	Griggs	W	"		"					
1596	C/Sgt	Lewis	G L	MG		"					
826	Rfn	Pratt	H B	"		"					
1972	A/C	Brindley	J T	D		"					
7240	Rfn	Brown	C	"		"					
7228	"	Carrshed	P B	"		"					
2838	A/C	Head	W E	"		"					
5103	"	Laughlen	W	"		"					
1592	Sgt	Dyson	E	C		"					[illegible] 23rd Buried L22 D C 3 [illegible]

CASUALTY RETURN

Regtl No	Rank & Name			Coy	Killed	Wounded	Slightly wounded at duty	Gassed		Evacuated	Remarks
3425	A/c	Cook	H J	C		26.7.15					
7166	Rfn	Steptoe	A	"		"					
6219	"	Collier	E	D		"					
6217	"	Thiel	W	C		"					
3355	"	Wain	A	"		"					
3052	"	Ferns	S	"		"					
1435	A/c	Tomkinson	G	"		"					
871	Sgt	Saunders	P	D		"					
2133	Cpl	Brown	R W	A		"					
2073	Rfn	Hopkins	C	D		"					
3127	Cpl	Todd	A E	"		"					
1599	Rfn	Archer	R	"		"					
5072	"	Gout	C	A		"					
637	"	Cox	W H	D		"					
2573	A/c	Allbutt	F	A		"					
3235	Sgt	Williams	R	C		"					

CASUALTY RETURN

RECTL No	RANK AND NAME			COY	KILLED	WOUNDED	SLIGHTLY WOUNDED AT DUTY	GASSED			REMARKS
1975	Rfn	Standing	C	D		24/7/15					
2258	"	Ross	J	C		"					
2133	"	Symons	F			"					
393	"	Jones	C W	A		"					
1603	"	Burd	W E	C		"					
2092	"	Berry	G	D		"					
2427	"	Eaton	W	C		"					
3417	"	Sparrow	C H			"					
1239	"	Feld	A	D		"					
3104	"	Topham	J	"		"					
~~2277~~	"										
528	"	Thom	W C	A		"					
2277	Rfn	Norton	J	C	25.7.15						Field Hedges
446	"	Atole	A V	A	"						
3022	C/L	Gooding	G B	"	"						Crater House

CASUALTY RETURN.

REGTL No.	RANK	AND NAME		COY	KILLED	WOUNDED	SLIGHTLY WOUNDED AT DUTY	GASSED			REMARKS
22	Cpl	Hutchinson	A J	A	25.7.15						Field nr Ardoy
5174	Rfn	Chuck	F E	"	"						"
395	"	Harris	G	C	"						"
1896	"	Steele	A	A	"						"
529	"	Johnston	R	"		25.7.15			Died of wounds 25th		"
340	A/C	Summerhalt	W A	"		"					
468	Rfn	Smith	C H	"		"					
528	"	Thorne	W E	"		"					
614	"	Eldridge	J	C		"					
2768	"	Morland	J	"		"					
2669	"	Sotheran	W H	"		"					
3033	"	Wroe	H	"		"					
5121	"	Redding	C	D		"					
5106	Rfn	Turner	W	B		26/7/15			Died of Wounds 26th		Field nr Ardoy
5094	"	Costar	W	"		"					

CA[illegible]UALTY RETURN

REGT. No	RANK	NAME		COY	KILLED	WOUNDED	SLIGHTLY wounded at duty	GASSED			Remarks
1856	C/pl	Cleveland	WH	D		26-7-15					
9406 ~~[illegible]~~	Sgt	Vallis	HR	B		"					
1512	Rfn	Pilkeathley	T	B		21 7.15					
2494	"	Lord	G	"		"					
452	A/c	Mills	C	"		"					
3435	Rfn	Ashmore	HF	C		"					
831	Rfn	Cooper	C	B		27-7-15					
716	"	Ridley	T	"		"					
2432	"	Frost	CG	C		"					
6599	Rfn	Wilde	L	D		28/7/15					
9289	"	Martin	R	"		"					
9207	"	Smith	G	"		"					
645	"	Luck	HA	B		"					

CASUALTY RETURN

REGTL No.	RANK & NAME			Coy	KILLED	WOUNDED	SLIGHTLY WOUNDED AT DUTY	GASSED			REMARKS
2687	Rf.	Stennett	W.	D		28-7-15					
9454	"	Weekes	W	"		"					
8382	A/c	Parslow	G	"		"					
10465	Rf.	Jones	W.G	"		"					
827	"	Fraser	W.A	B		"					
2425	"	Prince	G.T	C		"					
707	"	Lloyd	I.L	B		"					
2661	"	Tomlinson	W.	C		"					

1

Regtl No.	Rank & Name		Coy	Killed	Wounded	Slightly wounded at duty	GASSED	MISSING	~~Evacuated~~ DIED OF WOUNDS	Remarks
B3415	A/Sgt	Hunter D. J.	C	30-7-15						
B3422	Rfn	Beer H. A	"	"						
~~[illegible]~~	—	~~[illegible] J~~	—	—						
B3421	"	Jackson F.	"	"						
B3414	"	Knight A. N. S	"	"						
11737	"	Mills C.	"	"						
Capt.	P.	Collins	"	"						
Lieut.	G. W. L	Talbot	"	"						
2nd Lt	G. F. C.	Devitt	"						30-7-15	
B3454	Rfn	Limby P. L.	"	30.7.15						
B2209	"	Moulding	"	"						
B3440	"	Reader C. L	"	"						
8698	C.S.M	Edwards G	"		30.7.15					
B3412	Sgt	Chumley J. L.	"		"					
B3392	"	Herd W. E	"		"					

Regt No.	Rank	Name	Coy	Killed	Wounded	Wounded slightly at duty	Gassed	Missing	DIED OF WOUNDS	Remarks
B651	Sgt	Smith M.	C		30.7.15					
8663	"	Tedder A. J.	"		"				31-7-15	Buried Sheet 27. L22 3.6.3
B1669	Cpl	Kenchatt R	"		"					
B3447	"	Binet F	"		"					
B1756	A/Cpl	Davis H.	"		"					
B1684	"	Elkes C.W.	"		"					
B3937	Rfn	Aldridge S.G.	"		"					
B2656	"	Anstee F	"		"					
S7335	"	Ayling Y.	"		"				8-8-15	Reported from Base LIVERPOOL MERCHANTS' MOBILE H'TAL ETAPLES
S7182	"	Berry J.	"		"					
S8576	"	Bartlett J	"		"					
~~B6[illegible]~~	~~"~~	~~Eldridge J~~	~~"~~		~~"~~					
B3206	Rfn	Beddows B	C		30.7.15					
B1583	"	Bedworth A	"		"					
B2125	"	Benjamin W	"		"					

31

Regtl No.	Rank	Name	Coy	Killed	Wounded	Wounded slightly at duty	Gassed	Missing	Died of wounds	Remarks
B1894	Rfn	~~[illegible]~~ Boorer J	C		30-7-15					
B3517	Cpl	Robotham A W	"		"					
B3474	Rfn	Bone A	"		"					
B636	"	Boyd W	"		"					
B2434	"	Clements A	"		"					
B1911	"	Collins G	"		"					
B3337	"	Costello R	"		"					
B3438	"	Cowley J.A	"		"					
B3475	"	Curtiss J. W	"		"					
S7183	"	Compton S	"		"					
S9752	"	Davis J	"		"					
B2918	"	Dangerfield S C	"		"					
B3466	"	Dent W	"		"					
B3456	"	Deryck A	"		"					
B2927	"	Eaton W	"		"					

Regtl No	Rank	Name	Coy	Killed	Wounded	Wounded slightly at duty	Gassed	Missing	Died of wounds	Remarks
B/4909	Rfn	Freer F	C		30.7.15					
B/3372	"	Frith J	"		"					
B/3519	"	Gaskin C	"		"					
B/3424	"	Gibbs R.J	"		"					
B/3227	"	Gray A	"		"					
B/86	a/C	Hankey D.W	"		"					
B/1662	Rfn	Handley T	"		"					
B/3512	a/Cpl	Hanmer A.J	"		"					
B/3915	Rfn	Hardy H	"		"					
B/3577	"	Heath J	"		"					
B/2833	"	Hicks W.	"		"					
B/1819	"	Howard R	"		"					
B/1823	"	Howarth E	"		"					
B/2441	"	Ingram J	"		"					
B/3463	"	Jacobs C	"		"					

5

Regtl No	Rank	Name	Coy	Killed	Wounded	Wounded Slightly at duty	Gassed	Missing	Died of Wounds	Remarks
B 2316	Rfn	Jones W. G	C		30.7.15					
S 6207	"	Jesoop A	"		"					
B 3945	"	Kelly E	"		"					
B 1667	"	Kenchatt R	"		"					
B 3430	"	Lewis F. C	"		"					
B 3936	"	Lovett J	"		"					
B 2831	"	Lillystone J	"		"					
B 1907	A/Cpl	Massey A	"		"					
S 7181	Rfn	Norton J	"		"					
B 3489	"	Nash G	"		"					
B 3237	"	Noyce E	"		"					
B 2057	"	Owen J	"		"					
B 6050	"	Parsons T. G	"		"					
B 2835	"	Robinson G	"		"					
B 3443	"	Salter T.	"		"					

Regtl No	Rank	Name	Coy	Killed	Wounded	Wounded & remained at duty	~~Missing~~ Gassed	Missing	Died of Wounds	Remarks
B3976	Rfn	Stait C	C		30.7.15					
B1668	A/Cpl	Giles F.W	"		"					
C1757	Rfn	Luck A	"		"					
B1995	"	Tapling B	"		"					
B3391	"	Thomas J.A	"		"					
B1683	"	Wyatt S	"		"					
S6058	"	Webb. A	"		"					
B3212	"	Yates W	"		"					
Z 1	A/Cpl	Langley A	"		"				31-7-15	Buried Sheet 27 L 22 D 6.3
S11796	Rfn	Spicer W	"		"					
S6011	"	Williams J	"		"					
S9762	"	Staines L.H	"		"					
S6983	"	Rogers A	"		"					
S8429	"	Winch G	"		"					
S9588	"	Harris J	"		"					

7

Regtl No.	Rank	& Name	Coy	Killed	Wounded	Wounded slightly at duty	Gassed	Missing	Died of Wounds	
S 7579	Rfn	Hermann C	C.		30.7.15					
S 9303	"	Owen W	"		"					
S 2365	"	Page C	"		"					
B 2062	"	Anglinetta C	"		"					
Capt.	S.H.	Drummond.	"					30.7.15		
B. 2493	Rfn.	Beard W.	"					"		
B 1821	"	Dearden H.	"					"		
B 3419	"	Faulkner C	"					"		
S 7510	"	Goldney B.	"					"		
S 7176	"	Knowles J.	"					[illegible]	31.7.15	Buried Sheet 27. L.22 D 6.5.
B 3461	"	O'Key. J.	"		30.7.15					
B. 3378	"	Robertson W.	"		"					
B 2435	"	Sharples C.	"		"					
B 1901	"	Staggs C	"					30.7.15.		
B 3467	"	Taylor C	"					"		

Regtl. No.	Rank & Name.			Killed	Wounded	Wounded slightly at duty	Gassed	Missing	Died of Wounds
B 3460	Rfn.	Tomkins G.	C.					30.7.15	
B 3423	"	Undy A. S.	"					"	
S 7158	"	Haggar J.	"					"	
B 2070	Cpl.	Martin F. T.	B.					"	
S 6170	Rfn.	Briggs H.	"		30.7.15				
S 5155	"	Ashton W.	"		"				
B 5143	"	Brampton F.	"					30.7.15.	
S 8154	"	Byrne T.	"		30.7.15				
B. 1980	"	Chatwin G. W.	"					30.7.15	
S 8686	"	Bradford T.	"					"	
B. 1366	"	Davenport J.	"		30.7.15.				
B 929	"	Merrigan F. G.	"					30.7.15	
B 832	"	Phillips T.	"					"	
B 1358	"	Price P.	"					"	
B 1448	"	Sanderson W.	"					"	

Regtl. No.	Rank & Name			Killed	Wounded	Slightly wounded at duty	Gassed	Missing	Died of Wounds	
B.1984	Rfn.	Smith H.	B.		30.7.15					
B 628	"	Taylor J.	"		"					
B/1304	"	Taylor R.	"		"					
S 6208	"	Warder R. G.	"					30.7.15.		
B 754	"	Webb. D.	"		30.7.15					
S 6222	"	Wooster W.	"		"					
B 1445	"	Taylor W.	"		"					
B 1528	"	Williams H.	"					30.7.15.		
B 712	C/Sgt	Bonham A.	"		30.7.15					
2nd. Lt.	J. E.	Marriott	"	30.7.15						
B 1434	Cpl.	Ridings W.	"	"						
S 7167	a/Cpl.	Cowley A. V.	"		30.7.15.					
B 1513	Rfn.	Doyle W.	"	30.7.15						
A 1445	"	Buck H.	"	"						
A. 2495	"	Hoselton G.	"	"						
S 5144	"	Groves D.	"	"						

Regtl. No.	Rank & Name			Killed	Wounded	Slightly wounded at duty	Gassed	Missing	Died of Wounds	
S11688	Rfn.	Gifford C.	B.	30.7.15						
S11713	"	Jacobs A.	"	"						
B 643	"	Laveday W.	"	"						
A1453	"	Townsend A.E.	"	"						
Capt.	Hon.	C. S. Finch	"		30.7.15					
2nd Lt.	R. H.	Lawson.	"		"					
S7900	C.S.M.	Cole J. B.	"		"					
A4767	Sgt.	Fairhead E.	"		"					
B3956	"	Hoffman C.	"		"					
A1438	a/Sgt.	Cutterbar C.	"		"					
A622	Cpl.	Methven W.	"		"					
B1305	"	Smith J. E.	"		"					
B3219	"	West A. R.	"		"					
B1368	"	Nash J.	"		"					
B1436	a/Cpl.	Martin H. W.	"		"					
B1379	"	Burgess S.	"		"					

Regtl. No.	Rank & Name.			Killed	Wounded	Wounded Slightly at duty	Gassed	Missing	Died of Wounds.	
S 8768	Rfn.	Angel P.	B.		30.7.15					
B 2585	"	Bates J.	"		"					
B 1299	"	Beech J.	"		"					
B 819	"	Bird J.	"		"					
S 11615	"	Bowles D.	"		"					
B 1451	"	Bankester J.	"		"					
B 1352	"	Binks W.	"		"					
B 621	"	Bloomberg J.	"		"					
B 706	"	Callis J.	"		"					
B 1525	"	Davies S.	"		"					
B 1441	"	Dickson A.	"		"					
S 7387	"	Castiglione J.	A.		"					
S 6129	"	Craxton G.J.	"		"					
B 1511	"	Gilbert L.	"		"					
S 8687	"	Fowler C.	"		"					
S 672	"	Gray H.	"		"					

Regtl. No.	Rank & Name.			Killed	Wounded	Slightly Wounded at duty	Gassed	Missing	Died of Wounds
S 6054	Rfn.	Gray. J.	B.		30.7.15.				
R. 606	"	Hicks G. H.	"		"				
1659	"	Griffith T.	"		"				
1298	"	Foster J.	"		"				
3103	"	Hawley T.	"		"				
703	"	Jenkins R. F.	"		"				
S 7341	"	Jones E. G.	"		"				
1284	"	Long A. G.	"		"				
632	"	Matthews J.	"		"				
77	"	Milward T.	"		"				
2837	"	Malloy C.	"		"				
2505	"	McLaughlin T.	"		"				
830	"	Parkinson E.	"		"				
S 7168	"	Mall J.	"		"				
1360	"	Postlethwaite	"		"				
S 5109.	"	Pears. E.	"		"				

Regtl. No.	Rank & Name.			Killed	Wounded	Slightly Wounded at duty	Gassed	Missing	Died of Wounds	
B 2431	Rfn.	Prosser W.	B.		30.7.15					
B. 718	"	Platt. A. G.	B		"				31-7-18	Buried Sheet 27. L 22 I 6.B.
S 5063.	"	Russell G. A.	"		"					
S 5183	"	Simonds A. H.	"		"					
B 1449	"	~~[illegible]~~ Smith E.C.	"		"					
B 2358	"	Harris W.	"		"					
B 1514		Hanmer. W.	"		"					
B 631		Pattison J.	"		"					
S 5088		Penniment J.	"		"					
B 456		Peters A.	"		"					
B 623		Wilson J.	"		"					
B 750		Slaw W.	"		"					
B 1290		Stevens J.	"		"					
B 647		Tweed B.	"		"					
B 1446		Townsend J.	"		"					
B 1263		Wall W.	"		"					

Regtl. No.	Rank & Name.			Killed	Wounded	Slightly Wounded at duty	Gassed	Missing	Died of Wounds	
S 7327	Rfn.	Young H.	B.		30.7.15.					
B 746	Cpl	Webb. B. J.	"		"					
B 2922	Rfn.	Nichols W.	"		"					
B 818	"	Clarke W.	"		"					
B 2357	a/Cpl.	Chatwin W. J.	"		"					
B 641	Rfn.	Thompson A	"		"					
S 11763	"	McDonald J	"		"					
Capt.	W. R.	Mc Ilwaine	D.		"					
2nd. Lt.	A.	Godsal.	"	30.7.15.						
B 790	Cpl.	Hopkins C.	"		30.7.15					
B 1593	"	Hulton C.	"		"					
B 5065	a/Cpl.	Crofts J.	"		"					
S 7587	"	Gibson A.	"		"					
B 2053	"	Allen J.	"		"					
B 2572	"	Greatbanks A	"	30.7.15						
B 2065	"	Pearce C.	"		30.7.15.					

Regtl. No.	Rank & Name.			Killed	Wounded	Slightly Wounded at duty	Gassed	Missing	Died of Wounds.
B 2693	Rfn.	Bishop J.	B.		30.7.15				
B 1661	"	Brown J.	"					30.7.15	
B 1674	"	Bunn W.	"		30.7.15				
B 1768	"	Ellis H.	"					30.7.15	
B 2849	"	Farrell J.	"		30.7.15				
B 2588	"	Hardy J.	"					30.7.15	
B 2077	"	Hogg P.	"		30.7.15				
S 7245	"	Hills P. E.	"		"				
B 2586	"	Jared C.	"		"				
B 2829	"	King J.	"	30.7.15					
B 1673	"	Lidster E. L.	"					30.7.15	
B 1998	"	McBurnie C.	"					"	
B 2207	"	Noton J.	"		30.7.15				
B 2348	"	Smith H.	"		"				
B 1971	"	Stott B.	"		"				
S 5161	"	Thripp W.	"		"				

Regtl. No.	Rank & Name			Killed	Wounded	Slightly wounded at duty	Gassed	Missing	Died of Wounds	
B 2440	Rfn.	Webb. S.	B.		30.7.15					
S 9528.	"	Bathgate J.	"		"					
S 9434	"	Childs H.	"		"					
S 9558	"	Jackson H.	"		"					
Z 147	Sgt.	Blears H.	"		"					
S 9735	Rfn.	Hockham	"		"					
B 2272	"	Sime F.	"		"					
S 5120	"	Winder W.	"					30.7.15		
S 9508	"	Phillips F.	"		30.7.15					
B 923	"	Underwood B	"		"					
S 9454	"	Weeks W.	"					30.7.15		
B 184	Sgt.	King E. G.	A		30.7.15.					
B 57	"	Chinchen W.	"		"					
S 7584	a/cpl.	Holland W.	"		"					
B 10	Cpl.	Wainsborough R.	"		"					
B 78	Sgt.	McCarthy J. J.	"		"					

7

Regtl. No.	Rank & Name.		Coy	Killed	Wounded	Slightly Wounded at duty.	Gassed.	Missing	Died of Wounds.	
B 101	L/Cpl.	Foster S. J.	A		30.7.15					
B 2574	"	Spong H.	"		"				29.8.15	Reported from No 23 Gen. H'tal.
B 183	Rfn.	Aldis S. W.	"		"					
B 2063	"	Thompson A.	"		"					
B 261	"	Gordon H.	"		"					
B 246	"	Stoner A. E.	"		"					
B 3363	"	McMillan R.	"		"					
B 7391	"	Harris C.	"		"					
B 7392	"	Harris R.	"					30.7.15		
B 347	"	Denton J.	"		30.7.15					
B 402	"	Quinney W.	"		"					
B 294	"	Smith A. J.	"		"					
B 151	"	Ralph C.	"		"					
B 245	"	Reeves J.	"		"					
B 5088	L/Cpl.	Warren R.	"	30.7.15.						
B 620	Rfn	Smith W. G.		"						

Regtl. No.	Rank	Name	Coy.	Killed	Wounded	Slightly wounded at duty	Gassed	Missing	Died of wounds.
B 438	A/Cpl.	Bodman J. B.	A.		•			30.7.15	
B 362	Rfn.	Newall W.	"		30.7.15.				
B 300	"	Taylor H. A.	"					30.7.15.	
B 308	A/Cpl.	Stone J.	"		30.7.15.				
B 3362	Rfn.	Holmes G. H.	"					30.7.15.	
S 5180.	"	Fowler W.	"					"	
B 190	"	Brown C. G.	"		30.7.15.				
S 7345	"	Watts J.	"					30.7.15.	
S 11759	"	Scates A	"		30.7.15.				
S 5681	"	Annett R	"		"				
B 339	"	Copeland A	"		"				
S 5941	"	Olver W. G.	"		"				
B 1522	"	Taylor E.	"		"				
~~B 379~~	"	~~Parry H~~	"						
~~S 5006~~	"	~~Jeffery A~~	"						
~~[illegible]~~	"	~~[illegible]~~	"						

Regtl. No.	Rank & Name		Coy.	Killed	Wounded	Wounded at duty	Gassed	Missing	Died of Wounds	
Capt.	P. H.	Milward	A		30.7.15					
"	2. B. H.	Drummond	"		"					
Lt.	J. H.	Foxshill	"						30.7.15.	
B2847	C/Cpl.	White C. M	C		30.7.15					
C1679	Rfn	Reilton H	"		"					
S6170	"	Briggs H	B		"					
S7325	"	Buck P	"		"					
S7405	"	Dingain J. J.	"		"					
S9334	"	Edwards A. J	A		"					
S8092	"	Hathing H	B		"					
S5189	"	Hodges J	"		"					
B3413	Cpl.	Hunt D.	C		"					
S7572	Rfn	Lunnigs G	D		"					
B2515	"	Moore C. A	C		"					
B2431	"	Prosser W	B		"					
S7146	"	Roberts E	C		"					

Regtl No.	Rank & Name		Coy	Killed	Wounded	Wounded Slightly at Duty	Gassed	Missing	Died of Wounds	Remarks
S10326	Rfn	Whittell J.	C		30.7.15					
B1979	A/Cpl	Walker J	B		"					
S8319	Rfn	O'Brien D	A		"					

41/14th Division

131/6300

7th K.R.R.C.

Vol III 1.7. — 2.8.15.

Confidential

War Diary of

7th (Service) Bn.

King's Royal Rifle Corps.

From 1st July 1915 to

2nd August 1915

Instructions regarding War Diaries and Intelligence Summaries are contained in F. S. Regs., Part II. and the Staff Manual respectively. Title pages will be prepared in manuscript.

WAR DIARY

~~or~~

~~INTELLIGENCE~~ SUMMARY.

(~~Erase heading not required.~~)

Army Form C. 2118.

Place	Date	Hour	Summary of Events and Information	Remarks and references to Appendices
[illegible]	[illegible]		[illegible]	

Page 5

Instructions regarding War Diaries and Intelligence Summaries are contained in F. S. Regs., Part II. and the Staff Manual respectively. Title pages will be prepared in manuscript.

WAR DIARY
~~or~~
~~INTELLIGENCE~~ SUMMARY.

(Erase heading not required.)

Army Form C. 2118.

Place	Date	Hour	Summary of Events and Information	Remarks and references to Appendices
Trenches opposite BELLE WAARDE FARM E. of YPRES	8.7.15		Battn in same trenches. Relieved during the night by 42nd Inf. Bde. Casualties 2 killed 7 wounded. The whole of this tour of duty in the trenches was marked by considerable German artillery activity. Support trenches were constantly shelled, the position being enfiladed by a German gun of heavy calibre, probably 8", fired from WYTSCHAETE. Free use was made of gas shells particularly against Bn Hd Qrs. No serious damage was caused by the gas in these.	
2 miles W. of POPERINGHE	9.7.15		Battn reached billets about 8 A.M. Resting.	
"	10.7.15		Same billets. Working party casualties 2 wounded.	
"	11.7.15		" " " " 1 "	
"	12.7.15		" " Coys. at drill route marching etc.	
"	13.7.15		" "	
"	14.7.15		"	
"	15.7.15		"	
"	16.7.15		"	
"	17.7.15		" 1 killed 2 wounded.	
"	18.7.15		" " " "	[illegible]

Instructions regarding War Diaries and Intelligence Summaries are contained in F. S. Regs., Part II. and the Staff Manual respectively. Title pages will be prepared in manuscript.

WAR DIARY

~~or~~

~~INTELLIGENCE~~ SUMMARY.

(Erase heading not required.)

Army Form C. 2118.

Place	Date	Hour	Summary of Events and Information	Remarks and references to Appendices
2 miles W of POPERINGHE	19.7.15		[illegible]	
"	20.7.15		[illegible]	
"	21.7.15		[illegible]	[illegible]
"	22.7.15		[illegible]	
"	23.7.15			
VLAMERTINGHE	24.7.15		[illegible]	[illegible]
"	25.7.15			
"	26.7.15			
"	27.7.15			
"	28.7.15			
"	29.7.15		[illegible]	
[illegible]	30.7.15		Relief of 8th [illegible] Rifles [illegible] at [illegible]	
		[illegible]	attack by Germans [illegible]	
			[illegible] on left lost. B Coy. [illegible] to [illegible] G 3 [illegible]	
			[illegible] down G 3 [illegible]	
			day. Trench F1 lost but retaken by D Coy. [illegible]	

1577 Wt. W10791/1773 500,000 1/15 D. D. & L. A.D.S.S./Forms/C 2118.

Page 7

WAR DIARY
~~or~~
~~INTELLIGENCE SUMMARY.~~

(*Erase heading not required.*)

Instructions regarding War Diaries and Intelligence Summaries are contained in F. S. Regs., Part II. and the Staff Manual respectively. Title pages will be prepared in manuscript.

Army Form C. 2118.

Place	Date	Hour	Summary of Events and Information	Remarks and references to Appendices
HOOGE	30.7.15 continued		killed or driven out 2/Lieut LONGBOTTOM in command being killed – News gradually reaches Bn HdQrs. that Lt. SEYMOUR ROBINSON. CAPT. DOWLING. LT ARNELL are killed CAPT. RADCLIFFE mortally wounded. CAPT. EVANS & 2 Lieut. LAWRENCE are wounded & that there are many casualties in other ranks. There are at this time 2 platoons of D Coy. 1 platoon of B Coy. in support & matters appeared serious when 8 K.R. Rifles who had turned round & marched straight back from their intended billets began to arrive. They had been had no sleep & no food. Our own battalion was in the same position – Eventually orders were received that an artillery bombardment would begin at 2 p.m & an infantry counter	[illegible]
		2 pm 2.45 pm	attack would be made at 2.45 p.m. This was duly carried out. The infantry counter attack failed being brought to a standstill by heavy machine gun fire shell fire & rifle fire. Many casualties occurred & there were at the moment only 2 platoon commanders left in the Bn viz: 2/Lieut FRANCIS & LT. WILLIAMSON the other company officers being CAPT. WORMALD. LATERRIERE & WARRE. 2/Lieut ROE turned up about this time having been away on a course. He heard of the fight & rejoined. As it was getting dusk orders were received that the Batn would be relieved by 6 D.C.L.I. The relief was duly effected under cover of darkness & the men were withdrawn. [illegible] 92 which had been held all day was ordered to be abandoned. The casualties sustained by the	

1577 Wt. W10791/1773 500,000 1/15 D. D. & L. A.D.S.S./Forms/C. 2118.

Instructions regarding War Diaries and Intelligence Summaries are contained in F. S. Regs., Part II. and the Staff Manual respectively. Title pages will be prepared in manuscript.

WAR DIARY

~~or~~

~~INTELLIGENCE SUMMARY.~~

(Erase heading not required.)

Army Form C. 2118.

Place	Date	Hour	Summary of Events and Information	Remarks and references to Appendices
HOOGE	30.7.15 (contd)		[illegible] Capt G. E. DOWLING, 2/Lt [illegible] SEYMOUR [illegible] R B ARNOLD [illegible] ROBINSON 2/Lt R LONGBOTTOM killed [illegible] B F CARTER died of wounds [illegible] RADCLIFFE missing believed [illegible] missing. Capt [illegible] A R EVANS [illegible] G H GIBSON [illegible] WORMALD [illegible] Capt H M B de SALIS [illegible] LA FERRIERE wounded [illegible] other ranks [illegible] 187 missing 17. The chief [illegible] of the day [illegible] against [illegible] (1) appears to have been [illegible] the 9th R B [illegible] which the Germans consolidated their position (3) the [illegible] bombardment [illegible] (4) the defence of G2 [illegible] by A [illegible] under CAPTS WORMALD [illegible] LA FERRIERE [illegible] without [illegible] [illegible] exposed to [illegible]	
1 mile E of POPERINGHE	31.7.15		Bn to bivouac arriving about 6 A.M. resting	
"	1.8.15		Same bivouac. reorganization of Coys. arrival of draft of 2 officers LT COOPER BLAND & 2/Lt [illegible] & [illegible] O.R.	
"	2.8.15		Same bivouac. Inspection by G.O.C. VI Corps.	[illegible]

1577 Wt. W10791/1773 500,000 1/15 D. D. & L. A.D.S.S./Forms/C. 2118.

14th Division

121/6607

7th K.R.R.C.

Vol: IV

From 1 - 31. 8. 15

Nil

Page 9.

Instructions regarding War Diaries and Intelligence Summaries are contained in F. S. Regs., Part II. and the Staff Manual respectively. Title pages will be prepared in manuscript.

WAR DIARY
~~or~~
~~INTELLIGENCE SUMMARY.~~
(*Erase heading not required.*)

Army Form C. 2118.

Place	Date	Hour	Summary of Events and Information	Remarks and references to Appendices
1 mile E. of POPERINGHE	1.8.15	"	Batn in bivouac - resting -	
"	2.8.15		" " " Inspection of batn by G.O.C. VIth Corps - 2 machine gun detachments to trenches with 8th K.R.R.C.	
"	3.8.15		" " " 2 casualties in machine gun detachment.	
"	4.8.15		" "	
"	5.8.15		" " Draft of 200 from 15th Bn. A+B Coys. made up to strength of 130 each to trenches in front of Y wood - Coys. come under orders of O.C. 5th Ox. & Bucks.	
"	6.8.15.		Batn in bivouac - 1 platoon new draft sent to reinforce A+B Coys.	
"	7.8.15		" " A+B Coys relieved during night of 7th/8th Aug. They were subjected to continuous & heavy fire from shells & trench mortars during their tour of duty. Their casualties were killed 10 - wounded - 34 -	
"	8.8.15		Batn in bivouac resting.	
"	9.8.15		" " " 2Lieut. J. H Roe who was on duty in the trenches in command of a trench mortar was reported killed. 400 men detailed to dig by day E. of VLAMERTINGHE.	
"	10.8.15		Batn in bivouac. 400 men digging same place. Bn ordered to move at 6 p.m. to bivouac 1 mile S.W. of WATOU. arriving about 9 p.m.	
1 mile SW of WATOU	11.8.15		Batn in bivouac - following officers joined Lt. C C OMMANNEY. 2Lt. E. H WALSHAM. F. W. RAMSAY. A. W. HOLINY. L. M R. McLAGLEN. C. R. D. PULLING. M. L R. ROMER. L. W. LEWIS. C. WHITLEY. E. PAGE. P. R. HAWORTH.	G S [illegible] Major 7 K.R.R.C.

1577 Wt. W10791/1773 500,000 1/15 D. D. & L. A.D.S.S./Forms/C. 2118.

Page 10

Instructions regarding War Diaries and Intelligence Summaries are contained in F. S. Regs., Part II. and the Staff Manual respectively. Title pages will be prepared in manuscript.

WAR DIARY
or
INTELLIGENCE SUMMARY.
(Erase heading not required.)

Army Form C. 2118.

Place	Date	Hour	Summary of Events and Information	Remarks and references to Appendices
1 mile S W of WATOU	12.8.15		Batt^n resting in [illegible]	
"	13.8.15		Batt^n paraded 5.30 p.m. & [illegible] by motor [illegible] [illegible] [illegible]	
Trenches E. of YPRES			N. of RAILWAY WOOD [illegible] 1 mile E. of YPRES	
"	14.8.15		Relief [illegible] 1.30 A.M. Quiet day in [illegible] A. C. D. Coys [illegible] [illegible] B [illegible]	
"	15.8.15		Trenches [illegible] 2 wounded.	
"	16.8.15		" [illegible] Quiet.	
"	17.8.15		" [illegible] 2 wounded.	
"	18.8.15		" 2 wounded.	
"	19.8.15		" 4 wounded.	
"	20.8.15		" 5 wounded.	
"	21.8.15		" 6 wounded.	
"	22.8.15		" 1 killed 2 wounded.	
"	23.8.15		" 3 wounded.	
"	24.8.15		" 1 officer (Lt. [illegible]) [illegible] 1 O.R. wounded. On the night of 24/25 the line was rearranged with the result that the Battalion was allotted a [illegible] D & B Coys in [illegible] line. C Coy in support in X line. A Coy in reserve in [illegible]	
"	25.8.15		Trenches Quiet day.	
"	26.8.15		" " "	
"	27.8.15		" 1 officer (2/Lt HALSHAM) wounded 9 other ranks. Draft of 77 other ranks received	[illegible] Major [illegible]

Page 11.

Instructions regarding War Diaries and Intelligence Summaries are contained in F. S. Regs., Part II. and the Staff Manual respectively. Title pages will be prepared in manuscript.

WAR DIARY
or
INTELLIGENCE SUMMARY.
(Erase heading not required.)

Army Form C. 2118.

Place	Date	Hour	Summary of Events and Information	Remarks and references to Appendices
Trenches E. of YPRES.	28.8.15.		Trenches: quiet day.	
"	29.8.15		" 1 wounded.	
"	30.8.15		Battalion relieved at night by 8th K.R. Rifles & proceeds to rest bivouac E. of WATOU. This tour of duty in the trenches was quiet & marked by no particular incident total casualties being 2 officers wounded. 3 O.R. killed 35 wounded.	
1/2 mile E. of WATOU	31.8.15.		Rest bivouac –	[illegible] Major 7 K.R. Rifles

1577 Wt. W10791/1773 500,000 1/15 D. D. & L. A.D.S.S./Forms/C. 2118.

14th Div

7th K. R. R. C.
Vol 5

Confidential.

7th (Service) Bn. King's Royal Rifle Corps.

—WAR. DIARY—

FROM

1st September 1915

To

31st October 1915.

Page 12

Instructions regarding War Diaries and Intelligence Summaries are contained in F. S. Regs., Part II. and the Staff Manual respectively. Title pages will be prepared in manuscript.

WAR DIARY
or
INTELLIGENCE SUMMARY.
(Erase heading not required.)

Army Form C. 2118.

Place	Date	Hour	Summary of Events and Information	Remarks and references to Appendices
½ mile E of WATOU.	[illegible]		Rest bivouac.	
	[illegible]		[illegible]	
	3.9.15		[illegible]	
			B: M [illegible]	
	4.9.15		B. [illegible]	
	5.9.15		B. [illegible]. Draft of 61 other ranks from England.	
[illegible] YPRES	[illegible]		[illegible]	
	7.9.15		[illegible] 2 Coys. in KAAI SALIENT & 2 coys. in houses in BRIELEN ROAD. B. [illegible] in BRIELEN Road. Casualties [illegible]	
	8.9.15		1 wounded.	
	9.9.15		1 wounded.	
	10.9.15			
	11.9.15			
	12.9.15		5 wounded.	
	~~12.9.15~~		[illegible] the battalion was employed in finding strong working parties [illegible] building [illegible]	
	13.9.15		Battalion moves to trenches A3 & A4 in relief of 7 R.B. about 8 p.m. Disposition: C Coy. in A3. D Coy. in A4. B Coy. in X2 in support. D Coy. [illegible] (under orders of [illegible]) in KAAI [illegible]	

1577 Wt. W10791/1773 500,000 1/15 D. D. & L. A.D.S.S./Forms/C. 2118.

Instructions regarding War Diaries and Intelligence Summaries are contained in F. S. Regs., Part II. and the Staff Manual respectively. Title pages will be prepared in manuscript.

WAR DIARY
or
INTELLIGENCE SUMMARY.
(*Erase heading not required.*)

Army Form C. 2118.

Place	Date	Hour	Summary of Events and Information	Remarks and references to Appendices
Trenches E. of YPRES.	14.9.15		Trenches. casualty 1 wounded.	
	15.9.15		"	
	16.9.15		" " 1 wounded.	
	17.9.15		" " 1 wounded.	
	18.9.15		"	
	19.9.15		" " 2 wounded.	
	20.9.15		" " 1 wounded.	
	21.9.15		" " 3 killed 11 wounded. Battalion moves to bivouac about 1 mile E. of POPERINGHE, being relieved by 2nd Durham L.I. This tour of duty was marked by constant violent bombardments of the German trenches. There was not much reply at first but after a few days the German reply was vigorous & caused the casualties shewn above.	
1 mile E. of POPERINGHE	22.9.15		Bivouac. 2 lieut. H. WALSHAM officially reported to have died of wounds.	
"	23.9.15		Bivouac.	
"	24.9.15		Bivouac. Battalion ordered to be ready to move at short notice. 2 lieuts. Hon. D. BUTLER. BARLOW. LEWIS. SCOTT-RUSSELL join.	
WHITE CHÂTEAU	25.9.15		Bivouac. Battn moves 4 p.m. to WHITE CHÂTEAU on MENIN ROAD 1 mile E. of YPRES in support of 42nd Bde. attack on BELLEWARDE FARM. Attack unsuccessful. 43rd Brigade relieve 42nd in trenches. 41st Bde. in support. Disposition of Battn. A & C coys. & Hd Qrs. in dug outs at WHITE CHATEAU. B & D coys. in work N. of MENIN Road about 300x distant. Casualties 1 wounded.	
"	26.9.15		Dugouts. 2 lieuts. R E PEMBERTON. B. M. ARNOLD. S. T. BIRD. W. W. PALMER join. Casualties 1 wounded.	[illegible]

1577 Wt. W10791/1773 500,000 1/15 D. D. & L. A.D.S.S./Forms/C. 2118.

Army Form C. 2118.

WAR DIARY
or
INTELLIGENCE SUMMARY.
(Erase heading not required.)

Instructions regarding War Diaries and Intelligence Summaries are contained in F. S. Regs., Part II. and the Staff Manual respectively. Title pages will be prepared in manuscript.

Place	Date	Hour	Summary of Events and Information	Remarks and references to Appendices
[illegible]	[illegible]		[illegible]	
	[illegible]		[illegible]	
	[illegible]		[illegible]	
	[illegible]		[illegible]	

1577 Wt. W10791/1773 500,000 1/15 D. D. & L. A.D.S.S./Forms/C. 2118.

Page 15.

WAR DIARY
or
INTELLIGENCE SUMMARY.
(Erase heading not required.)

Army Form C. 2118.

Instructions regarding War Diaries and Intelligence Summaries are contained in F. S. Regs., Part II. and the Staff Manual respectively. Title pages will be prepared in manuscript.

Place	Date	Hour	Summary of Events and Information	Remarks and references to Appendices
WHITE CHATEAU MENIN RD.	1.10.15		Dugouts.	
	2.10.15		Dugouts.	
	3.10.15		Dugouts.	
	4.10.15		Dugouts.	
	5.10.15		Dugouts. Casualties 1 wounded.	
	6.10.15		Battalion moved in evening to relieve 8th R.B. trenches A14 to A19. Right in front of Y wood facing ETANG DE BELLEWARDE. left on RAILWAY WOOD. Casualties 1 wounded.	
Trenches A14 & A19.	7.10.15		Trenches. Casualties 3 wounded.	
	8.10.15		" " 1 wounded.	
	9.10.15		" " 2 killed 2 wounded.	
	10.10.15		" " 1 " 7 "	
	11.10.15		" " 4 "	
	12.10.15		" – Position very heavily bombarded from about 5 p.m. to 7 p.m. Casualties 2 killed. 12 wounded. Casualties very small considering the amount of stuff put in. Parapets a good deal damaged. Most of casualties incurred in bringing up supports as the Germans had put a curtain of shrapnel in rear of the fire trenches & it looked as if they were going to attack. They did not move however.	
	13.10.15		Battalion relieved 11 p.m. by 9th Kings Royal Rifles. Casualties 1 wounded. Moved to huts W. of VLAMERTINGHE. During this tour Bn was disposed as follows C Coy on right. D Coy centre. B Coy left. On 11.10.15 A Coy relieved C who took over support trenches & R 4. The trenches owing to the fight on 25.9.15 were in a bad state when we came in but much work was done on which Brigadier complimented the Batt.	

1577 Wt. W10791/1773 500,000 1/15 D. D. & L. A.D.S.S./Forms/C. 2118.

Page 16

Instructions regarding War Diaries and Intelligence Summaries are contained in F. S. Regs., Part II. and the Staff Manual respectively. Title pages will be prepared in manuscript.

WAR DIARY
or
INTELLIGENCE SUMMARY.
(Erase heading not required.)

Army Form C. 2118.

Place	Date	Hour	Summary of Events and Information	Remarks and references to Appendices
Huts near VLAMERTINGHE	14.10.15 to 31.10.15		During this period the battalion remained at rest finding working parties by day & night up to the [illegible] In the course of [illegible] one man was wounded on 19.10.15. The time generally was [illegible] in drilling, musketry [illegible] (training) of bombers etc.	
			On 15.10.15 a draft of 70 [illegible] joined the battalion.	
			The total casualties of the battalion [illegible] to date of writing 31.10.15 have been [illegible] officers [illegible] O.R.	

[illegible signature]

1577 Wt. W10791/1773 500,000 1/15 D. D. & L. A.D.S.S./Forms/C. 2118.

14th Division

9th K.R.R.C.
Vol: 6

K

121
7724

Nov. 15

nil
enc.

Instructions regarding War Diaries and Intelligence Summaries are contained in F. S. Regs., Part II. and the Staff Manual respectively. Title pages will be prepared in manuscript.

WAR DIARY
or
INTELLIGENCE SUMMARY.
(Erase heading not required.)

Army Form C. 2118.

Place	Date	Hour	Summary of Events and Information	Remarks and references to Appendices
Huts near Vlamertinghe	1.11.15 to 2.11.15		Continued training	
	2.11.15		2Lt Scott-Russell invalided to England	
L Farm	3.11.15		H.Q. B Coy at L Farm – A Coy in F13. C in X Line – D Coy in Ramparts. lent to 16th Infantry Brigade for work & carrying parties	
	5.11.15		1 O.R. wounded	
Ypres	6.11.15		H.Q. moved to Ramparts. A Coy to cellars in YPRES. C Coy to KAAIE 2Lt C.A. McGarvin granted a Commission from being Signalling Sergeant. 1 O.R. wounded	
CANAL BANK	9.11.15		Battalion except C Coy moved to dugouts in CANAL BANK – 2 OR wounded	
B Huts Vlamertinghe	10.11.15	1 am.	On return of working parties B Coy moved to B. Huts Vlamertinghe & the remainder of the Battalion followed on night of 11th/12th Nov ~~[illegible] wounded on working parties~~	
B Huts Vlamertinghe	11.11.15 to 19th 11.15		The Battalion remained at rest drilling & training bombers etc. On 15th 2Lt C WHITLEY returned from wounds.	
Trenches B13 – 15 S13 – 15	19.11.15		Battalion moved in evening to relieve the 6th Suffolk Regt in Trenches B 13. 14. 15 & S 13. 14. 15 in FORWARD COTTAGE SALIENT – Trenches in very bad state – falling in owing to wet – only possible to hold isolated bays – practically no wire in front of the trenches – 8th R.B. on our left & 43rd I. Bde on our right	

Army Form C. 2118.

WAR DIARY
or
INTELLIGENCE SUMMARY.

(Erase heading not required.)

Instructions regarding War Diaries and Intelligence Summaries are contained in F. S. Regs., Part II. and the Staff Manual respectively. Title pages will be prepared in manuscript.

Place	Date	Hour	Summary of Events and Information	Remarks and references to Appendices

1577 Wt. W10791/1773 500,000 1/15 D. D. & L. A.D.S.S./Forms C. 2118.

7th Bn. K. R. Rifles

Casualties through Sickness during month of Nov. 1915.

	Officers	O.R.
Admitted to Hospital during month	1.	76

Of above number 45 were evacuated out of Divisional Area and

22 O.R. rejoined from Hospital.

[illegible] ary

[illegible] Royal
[illegible] [illegible]

[illegible] 15
[illegible]

Page 19

Instructions regarding War Diaries and Intelligence Summaries are contained in F. S. Regs., Part II. and the Staff Manual respectively. Title pages will be prepared in manuscript.

WAR DIARY
or
INTELLIGENCE SUMMARY.
(Erase heading not required.)

Army Form C. 2118.

Place	Date	Hour	Summary of Events and Information	Remarks and references to Appendices
A HUTS Vlamertinghe	Dec 1st to 4.12.15		Battalion resting - a great deal of rain. On Dec 1st 1 machine gunner was killed in trenches. 11 O.R. rejoined	
Trenches B13 etc	4.12.15		Relieved 8th RB in B13 Trenches as before.	
	5th		Trenches - shelled intermittently from 8am to 4pm. B10 [illegible] suffering somewhat heavily part of the trench being completely blown in. Owing to the continual wet the trenches are in a worse state than ever. Casualties 2Lt Bird S.T. slightly wounded 2 O.R. killed & 5 wounded -	
	6th		Slight shelling - 3 O.R. wounded.	
	7th		Quiet day. 1 O.R. rejoined	
	8th	5am	49th Divisional Artillery opened a bombardment on the German trenches N.W of MORTELDJE. Some retaliation in rear of our trenches	
		11am	Very heavy bombardment on our sector particularly on S14, some 600 shells falling on or about S14 between 11 and 12 noon. Firing then died away ceased at 6.45. Intermittent firing during the rest of the day - Relieved in the evening by 8th RB & went to dug outs in CANAL Bank H.Q. [illegible] Farm as on 22nd ult. 10 O.R. killed & 23 wounded. 14 O.R. rejoined	
A Camp W of Poperinghe	9th		Bn moved in the evening by train from Asylum to Poperinghe & marched to A Camp	

1577 Wt.W10791/1773 500,000 1/15 D. D. & L. A.D.S.S./Forms/C. 2118.

Instructions regarding War Diaries and Intelligence Summaries are contained in F. S. Regs., Part II. and the Staff Manual respectively. Title pages will be prepared in manuscript.

WAR DIARY
or
INTELLIGENCE SUMMARY.
(Erase heading not required.)

Army Form C. 2118.

Place	Date	Hour	Summary of Events and Information	Remarks and references to Appendices

1577 Wt. W10791/1773 500,000 1/15 D. D. & L. A.D.S.S./Forms/C. 2118.

Page 21

Instructions regarding War Diaries and Intelligence Summaries are contained in F. S. Regs., Part II. and the Staff Manual respectively. Title pages will be prepared in manuscript.

WAR DIARY
or
INTELLIGENCE SUMMARY.
(Erase heading not required.)

Army Form C. 2118.

Place	Date	Hour	Summary of Events and Information	Remarks and references to Appendices
B. Huts W. of Poperinghe	Dec 17th		Bn in Corps Reserve at B. Huts - Very wet & muddy -	
	18th		1 officer wounded accidentally - self inflicted -	
	19th		Germans made a gas attack about 3.30 am against 6th Div - Effect of gas felt at B. Huts - Bn held in instant readiness to move - Heavy bombardment on both sides - 1 OR removed to F.A. suffering from gas -	
	20th		Order for instant readiness to move cancelled -	
	24th		Draft of reinforcements 95 OR arrived from England -	
Glimpse Cottage Trenches	31st		Bn relieved 8th R.B. 43rd Bde on the left of the Bn - 8th K.R.R. on the right - Draft of reinforcements 38 OR arrived from England - 1 OR killed - 1 OR wounded	
	Jan 1st		1 OR wounded - Bn relieved by 7th R.B. - after a quiet tour -	
	3rd		2 OR wounded - Bn in billets at Poperinghe -	
	5th			
	7th		Draft of reinforcements 60 O.R. arrived from England	

A. Richards Major

December 1915.

Average weekly strength was — 867 Other Ranks.

	Officers	O.R.
During the month there were admitted to Hospital – – –	1	– 124
Discharged from Hospl	–	– 38
Sick evacuated from Divisional Area	1	– 67

The majority of cases evacuated were men suffering from "Trench Feet".

7th K.R.R.C.
Vol 8

14

41 Bde

[illegible]

[illegible]

1st Battalion [illegible]

[illegible]

Army Form C. 2118.

Instructions regarding War Diaries and Intelligence Summaries are contained in F. S. Regs., Part II. and the Staff Manual respectively. Title pages will be prepared in manuscript.

WAR DIARY
or
INTELLIGENCE SUMMARY.
(Erase heading not required.)

Place	Date	Hour	Summary of Events and Information	Remarks and references to Appendices
Glympse Cottage Trenches	Jan 8th		Relieved trenches E24 to E27 inclusive taking over partly from 7th RB and partly from 8th RB. Shropshire Light Infantry on left of Bn & 8th KRR on right - 3 OR wounded -	
	9th		1 OR killed 1 OR wounded	
	10th		8 OR wounded	
	11th		1 OR wounded 1 OR killed	
	12th		1 OR wounded - Bn relieved by 8 RB - Bn went into huts and tents in No 1 Camp 3 miles NE of Poperinghe - on the whole a good camp - Tour of duty in trenches from 9th to 12th - fairly quiet but more enemy artillery fire than on previous day -	
	16th		Bn relieved 8th RB in trenches E24 to E27 inclusive - 8th KRR on right - 42nd Inf. Bde on left - 1 OR killed 5 OR wounded -	
	17th		1 OR killed - 2 OR wounded	
	18th		2 OR wounded	
	19th		2 OR wounded	
	20th		1 OR wounded - a draft of 20 OR reinforcements joined -	

1577 Wt. W19791/1773 500,000 1/15 D. D. & L. A.D.S.S./Forms/C. 2118.

Instructions regarding War Diaries and Intelligence Summaries are contained in F. S. Regs., Part II. and the Staff Manual respectively. Title pages will be prepared in manuscript.

WAR DIARY
or
INTELLIGENCE SUMMARY.
(Erase heading not required.)

Army Form C. 2118.

Place	Date	Hour	Summary of Events and Information	Remarks and references to Appendices
	22		[illegible]	
	23		[illegible]	
	26		[illegible]	
	27		[illegible]	
	28		[illegible]	
	29		[illegible]	
	31		[illegible]	

[illegible]

January 1915

Average weekly strength was. Officers 25. OR 939

	OR
During the month there were admitted to Hospital	59
Discharged from Hospital	16
Evacuated from Divisional Area	25

1/2/16

G. Rennie. Lt Col
Comdg 7th K. R. Rifles

Confidential

7th (Service) Battalion

The King's Royal Rifle Corps.

War Diary

From 1st February 1916

To 29th February 1916

Army Form C. 2118.

WAR DIARY

~~or~~

~~INTELLIGENCE SUMMARY.~~

(*Erase heading not required.*)

Instructions regarding War Diaries and Intelligence Summaries are contained in F. S. Regs., Part II. and the Staff Manual respectively. Title pages will be prepared in manuscript.

Place	Date	Hour	Summary of Events and Information	Remarks and references to Appendices
Popperinghe	Feb 1st		Bn relieved by 8th RB and went to billets in Popperinghe	
	2		2/Lt B. M. Arnold wounded whilst with Machine Gun Section – this officer afterwards died of wounds –	
	3		3 OR wounded	
	4		1 OR wounded – Draft of 8 OR reinforcements joined –	
	6		2/Lt A. L. Mackenzie joined Bn 2/Lt B M Arnold Died of Wounds	
	7		Bn relieved 8th RB in Trenches 24 to 27 inclusive – owing to Bn Hd Qrs at Glympse Cottage being blown in – Bn Hd Qrs were established on the Yser Canal Bank near Bridge 6 –	
	9		Captain A. P. Forster wounded whilst acting as Bde M. G. Officer. 1 OR killed	
	10		2/Lt J. G. Durham joined the Bn – 1 OR wounded in Popperinghe – Bn relieved by 8th RB night of 9/10 and proceeded to B Huts –	
BRIEL	11		Bn moved to billets in BRIEL 3 miles N of STEENWOORDE	
	14		Captain Gosling + Captain Fairlie rejoined battalion –	
			2/Lt G. H. Bailey joined Bn on promotion from Irish Guards –	

1577 Wt. W10791/1773 500,000 1/15 D. D. & L. A.D.S.S./Forms/C. 2118.

Army Form C. 2118.

Instructions regarding War Diaries and Intelligence Summaries are contained in F. S. Regs., Part II. and the Staff Manual respectively. Title pages will be prepared in manuscript.

WAR DIARY

or

~~INTELLIGENCE~~ SUMMARY.

(Erase heading not required.)

Place	Date	Hour	Summary of Events and Information	Remarks and references to Appendices
			2	

1577 Wt. W10791/1773 500,000 1/15 D. D. & L. A.D.S.S./Forms/C. 2118.

7th (Service) Bn. King's Royal Rifles.

February 1916.

The average weekly strength during the month Feb 1916 was 24 Officers. 950 Other Ranks.

During the month 2 Officers & 20 Other Ranks were admitted to Hospital of which 1 Officer & 14 O.R. evacuated the Divisional Area & 3 Other Ranks rejoined the Battalion.

[illegible] Capt.

Comdg 7th K.R. Rifles

Feb 1916.

7/KRRC
WO 95/1

7th (Service) Battalion.

The King's Royal Rifle Corps.

War Diary :—

From 1st March 1916

To 31st March 1916

To
The A.G's. Office at
the Base

Instructions regarding War Diaries and Intelligence Summaries are contained in F. S. Regs., Part II. and the Staff Manual respectively. Title pages will be prepared in manuscript.

WAR DIARY
~~or~~
~~INTELLIGENCE SUMMARY.~~
(Erase heading not required.)

Army Form C. 2118.

Place	Date	Hour	Summary of Events and Information	Remarks and references to Appendices
ARRAS	March 1.		The Battalion took over the BLANGY Sector – with 3 Coys in the front line – one Coy being lent by the 8th Bn King's Royal Rifles – from the 11th French Infantry Regt 6th Bde 33rd Division 17th Army Corps – our right was about 150 yards South of the CAMBRAI Road & our left on the River SCARPE. 7th Bn The Rifle Brigade was on our right. French Troops on our left – their right resting on the River SCARPE. their right being about 150 yds in rear of our left. They were relieved on the night of the 2/3rd by the 5th Division of the British Corps. The trenches are well made & in good, except the left sector, but falling in owing to the snow & frost. The left sector in the ruins of BLANGY Village had been very heavily shelled some 10 days ago when the French lost some small portion of their front line which makes the line extremely intricate.	
	2nd		1 O.R. wounded	
	3rd		2 O.R. wounded	
	4th		1 O.R. killed 6 O.R. wounded	
	5th		In the evening of today the 8th Bn Rifle Brigade relieved the attached Coy of the 8th KRRC & A Coy of this Battalion – thus shortening the line to a 3 Coy front. A Coy moved in to billets on the RUE de DOUAI in immediate support	

1577 Wt. W10791/1773 500,000 1/15 D. D. & L. A.D.S.S./Forms/C. 2118.

Instructions regarding War Diaries and Intelligence Summaries are contained in F. S. Regs., Part II. and the Staff Manual respectively. Title pages will be prepared in manuscript.

WAR DIARY

~~or~~

~~INTELLIGENCE~~ SUMMARY.

(Erase heading not required.)

Army Form C. 2118.

Place	Date	Hour	Summary of Events and Information	Remarks and references to Appendices

1577 Wt. W10791/1773 500,000 1/15 D. D. & L. A.D.S.S./Forms/C. 2118.

Instructions regarding War Diaries and Intelligence Summaries are contained in F. S. Regs., Part II. and the Staff Manual respectively. Title pages will be prepared in manuscript.

WAR DIARY

or

~~INTELLIGENCE~~ SUMMARY.

(*Erase heading not required.*)

Army Form C. 2118.

Place	Date	Hour	Summary of Events and Information	Remarks and references to Appendices
SIMENCOURT	20th		Battalion in Divisional Reserve – training etc. This was considerably interfered with by a sharp fall of snow on March 23rd & 24th	
ARRAS	25th		Marched to ARRAS & relieved 8th KRRC in I Sector. This again was a very quiet time & the weather being fine & warm the trenches were put in to first rate order. Communication trenches especially being much improved, and the defences of BLANGY greatly strengthened. Major A.P. EVANS seconded to command 41 Bde M.G. Coy.	
	26th		1 O.R. killed 2 O.R. wounded to duty. Captain J.W. LESLEY joined	
	27th		2Lt L.W. LEWIS (from wounds) & 2Lt G.H. EDWARDS joined	
	28th		3 O.R. wounded	
	29th		2 O.R. killed 1 O.R. wounded to duty – 2Lt J.N. MARTIN (A.S.C.) attached to Bn.	
	31st		1 O.R. wounded All casualties caused by snipers.	

1/4/1916.

G. Rennie. Lt. Col.
Comdg 7th Bn. K.R. Rifles

1577 Wt. W10791/1773 500,000 1/15 D. D. & L. A.D.S.S./Forms/C. 2118.

7th Bn. King's Royal Rifles

	O	OR
Average strength of Bn. during March 1916	25	960

During month 80 OR were admitted to Hospital sick.
Of these 23 were evacuated from Divisional Area, and 21 rejoined, the majority after a few days in Hospital.

G. Rennie. Lt Col.
Comdg 7th K. R. Rifles

1/4/16.

7th (Service) Battalion

The King's Royal Rifle Corps

War Diary

From 1st April 1916

To 30th April 1916

Army Form C. 2118.

Instructions regarding War Diaries and Intelligence Summaries are contained in F. S. Regs., Part II. and the Staff Manual respectively. Title pages will be prepared in manuscript.

WAR DIARY

~~or~~

~~INTELLIGENCE SUMMARY.~~

(Erase heading not required.)

Place	Date 1916	Hour	Summary of Events and Information	Remarks and references to Appendices
[illegible]	[illegible]		[illegible]	

1577 Wt. W10791/1773 500,000 1/15 D. D. & L. A.D.S.S./Forms/C. 2118.

7th (Service) Bn. King's Royal Rifles.

April 1916

During the month of April 1916 the average weekly strength was

28 Officers & 964 Other Ranks

There were 36 "Other Ranks" admitted to hospital during this month through sickness, 14 of these patients were evacuated out of the Divisional Area and 15 off them have now rejoined the Battalion.

G. Rennie. Lt. Col.
Comdg 7th K R Rifles

May 1916.

7th (Service) Battalion

The King's Royal Rifle Corps

War Diary

From 1st to 31st May 1916.

B.E.F.
1-6-1916.

XIV

Instructions regarding War Diaries and Intelligence Summaries are contained in F. S. Regs., Part II. and the Staff Manual respectively. Title pages will be prepared in manuscript.

WAR DIARY
or
INTELLIGENCE SUMMARY.
(Erase heading not required.)

Army Form C. 2118.

Place	Date	Hour	Summary of Events and Information	Remarks and references to Appendices
ARRAS I Sector Left TRENCHES	MAY 1st		Lt Hon. B.D. Butler struck off strength thro' sickness 28.4.16. 30 O.R. joined as reinforcements. Enemy opposite this sector very quiet & does not appear to be doing anything except defensive work.	
	3rd		Lt K.W. RAMSAY & 1 O.R. killed 1 O.R. wounded	
	4th		1 O.R. wounded. The Battalion was relieved by the 1st Bn EAST SURREY Regt of the 5th Division. On relief marched to huts at WANQUETIN for rest & training.	
WANQUETIN	6th		Lt J.N. MARTIN transferred from A.S.C.	
SAVY.	9		The Battalion marched to SAVY-BERLETTE going in to billets there. The ~~Battalion~~ Brigade being lent to the 17th Corps as Corps Reserve to be used for mining fatigues. Batt remained at SAVY training until 16th May	
MAROEUIL	16		Relieved the 8th R.B. H.Q. & 2 Coys at MAROEUIL. 1 Coy ANZIN: 1 Coy ROCLINCOURT all Coys employed on mining fatigues for 51st Div. MAJOR T.W.M. FUGE joined Bn: 2 Lt S.T. BIRD rejoined from wounds - draft of 14 O.R. joined	
	17		1 O.R. wounded	
	18		3 O.R. killed 4 O.R. wounded - Lt P.K. HAWORTH acc: wounded	
	19		1 O.R. wounded	
	21		1 O.R. wounded	
	22		1 O.R. wounded	
	23		1 O.R. wounded	
	24		1 O.R. wounded 30 O.R. joined	
	~~25~~			

1577 Wt. W10791/1773 500,000 1/15 D. D. & L. A.D.S.S./Forms/C. 2118.

Army Form C. 2118.

Instructions regarding War Diaries and Intelligence Summaries are contained in F. S. Regs., Part II. and the Staff Manual respectively. Title pages will be prepared in manuscript.

WAR DIARY
or
INTELLIGENCE SUMMARY.
(Erase heading not required.)

Place	Date	Hour	Summary of Events and Information	Remarks and references to Appendices
Mt St Eloy	May 25		[illegible] Mt St Eloy [illegible]	
	[illegible]		[illegible]	
	[illegible]		[illegible]	

1577 Wt. W10791/1773 500,000 1/15 D. D. & L. A.D.S.S./Forms/C. 2118.

7th (Service) Battalion

The King's Royal Rifle Corps.

May 1916.

The average strength of the Battalion during May 1916 was:–
32 Officers + 1000 Other Ranks.

---

1 Officer and 72 Other Ranks were admitted to Hospital during this period of which 33 Other Ranks rejoined the Battalion and 23 were evacuated out of the Divisional Area.

[illegible] Major

Comdg 7th K. R. Rifles

1/6/1916

June 7 K.R.R.C. Vol 13

XIV

Subject: War Diary. "Secret"

From
O.C. 7th Bn King's Royal Rifles

To
D.A.G.
3rd Echelon

B.E.F. 30th June 1916

Sir,

I beg to forward the original copy of the War Diary of the Battalion under my command for the period 1st to 30th June 1916.

G. Rennie Lt Col
Comdg 7th (Service) Battn
King's Royal Rifle Corps.

War Diary

of

The

7th (Service) Battalion

King's Royal Rifle Corps

From 1st June 1916

To 30th June 1916

Army Form C. 2118.

WAR DIARY

~~or~~

~~INTELLIGENCE~~ SUMMARY.

(Erase heading not required.)

Instructions regarding War Diaries and Intelligence Summaries are contained in F. S. Regs., Part II. and the Staff Manual respectively. Title pages will be prepared in manuscript.

Place	Date	Hour	Summary of Events and Information	Remarks and references to Appendices

1577 Wt. W10791/1773 500,000 1/15 D. D. & L. A.D.S.S./Forms/C. 2118.

Instructions regarding War Diaries and Intelligence Summaries are contained in F. S. Regs., Part II. and the Staff Manual respectively. Title pages will be prepared in manuscript.

WAR DIARY

~~or~~

~~INTELLIGENCE SUMMARY.~~

(Erase heading not required.)

Army Form C. 2118.

Place	Date	Hour	Summary of Events and Information	Remarks and references to Appendices
ROCLINCOURT	JUNE 24		Heavy firing some 15 miles South. Very quiet on our front. Lt G.H. GIBSON joined Bn on reposting. Germans fired 10 77mm Shrapnel at transport dump killing 1 O.R. & wounding 6 O.R. 2 of whom died of wounds.	
	25		Considerable artillery & trench mortar activity at 11.30 am by Bde on our left. Enemy retaliation weak. and again at 10.30 pm. at 11 pm our FA & Howitzers Trench Mortars & Machine Guns opened a sharp burst of rapid fire on Enemy front line & C.Ts. & again at 11.30 pm. Some 600 trench mortar Bombs were fired. The Germans did not reply. 2Lt DURHAM struck off strength from sickness. 2 O.R. wounded 1 O.R. died of wounds. Heavy firing South.	
	26		Sharp burst of fire & trench mortars by 152nd Bde at 10.30 am & again at 6 pm. 1 OR wounded. 1 OR accidentally wounded by bomb explosion.	
	27		The Germans would appear to have 1 Battery of 5.9's 1 of 4.2 Howitzers & 2 of 77 mm guns covering front held by 7th RB. Onwards & 152nd Bde. Relieved by 9th KRRC Completed at 3.40 am. Bn went into Billets in ST NICHOLAS. 1 Coy & Bn H.Q. 1½ Coys in ARRAS. 1 Coy in ROCLINCOURT. 1 Platoon in THELUS REDOUBT & 1 Platoon in OBSERVATORY Redoubt.	
ST NICHOLAS	28		Resting. Bn finds 200 odd men nightly for working parties	
	29		at 3 am 2 5.9" shells fell outside H.Q. wounding 4 O.R.	
	30		Resting	

G. Rennie Lt Col
Comdg 7. KRRC

1577 Wt. W10791/1773 500,000 1/15 D. D. & L. A.D.S.S./Forms/C. 2118.

7th (Service) Battalion
King's Royal Rifle Corps
June 1916

The average strength of the Battalion during June 1916 was:–
33 Officers & 1071 Other Ranks.

1 Officer & 41 Other Ranks were admitted to Hospital during the period of which 1 Officer and 12 Other Ranks rejoined the Battalion and 22 were evacuated out of the Divisional Area.

30/6/16

G. Rennie Lt-Col.
Comdg 7th K R Rifles

CONFIDENTIAL.

WAR DIARY

- of -

7 th Bn., KING'S ROYAL RIFLE CORPS.

From: 1st July, 1916.
To: 31st " 1916.

Volume. 15 ...

Army Form C. 2118.

Instructions regarding War Diaries and Intelligence Summaries are contained in F. S. Regs., Part II. and the Staff Manual respectively. Title Pages will be prepared in manuscript.

WAR DIARY
~~or~~
~~INTELLIGENCE~~ SUMMARY

(Erase heading not required.)

Place	Date	Hour	Summary of Events and Information	Remarks and references to Appendices
St NICHOLAS	July 1		[illegible] H.Q. [illegible]	
	2		[illegible]	
[illegible]	3		[illegible]	
	4		1 O.R. wounded [illegible]	
	5		[illegible] wounded	
	6		[illegible] wounded [illegible]	
	7		[illegible]	
DUISANS	10		[illegible]	
[illegible]	15		[illegible]	
	16		[illegible]	
	17		[illegible] killed	
	18		[illegible] wounded	
	19		1 O.R. wounded	
	20		1 O.R. wounded	
	21		[illegible]	
			[illegible] H.Q. [illegible] ARRAS [illegible]	
ARRAS			[illegible]	
	22		[illegible]	

2449 Wt. W14957/M90 750,000 1/16 J.B.C. & A. Forms/C.2118/12.

Instructions regarding War Diaries and Intelligence Summaries are contained in F. S. Regs., Part II. and the Staff Manual respectively. Title Pages will be prepared in manuscript.

WAR DIARY

~~or~~

~~INTELLIGENCE SUMMARY~~

(Erase heading not required.)

Army Form C. 2118.

Place	Date	Hour	Summary of Events and Information	Remarks and references to Appendices
ARRAS	July 23		Resting	
	24		Capt H.M. Gosling & CAPT E. FAIRLIE – ~~2Lt~~ 2Lt J.W. MARTIN wounded	
	25		1 O.R. Killed	
DUISANS	29		The Bn was relieved by the 9th K.O.Y.L.I. 21st Division & marched to bivouacs in DUISANS	
	30		marched to SUS ST LEGER parading at 9.50 am & arriving at 5 pm. an exceedingly hot & dusty march	
	31		no orders ~~received~~. Bn marched to OCCOCHES.	

31/7/1916.

G. Rennie Lt Col
Comdg 7th K.R. Rifles

1st Bn. Kings Royal Rifle Corps

During the month of July the number
Admitted to Hospital was 1 Officer 47 OR
of whom 27 OR were evacuated from
Divisional area and 9 OR rejoined

G. Pereira
Lieut Col
30.7.1916. Comdg 1st K.R.R.C.

14th Division.
41st Infantry Brigade.

1/7th BATTALION

KING'S ROYAL RIFLE CORPS

AUGUST 1 9 1 6

7th (Service) Bn. Kings Royal Rifle Corps

War Diary

From 1st August 1916

To 31st August 1916

Volume 16

Vol 15

7th (Service) Bn King's Royal Rifle Corps

Aug 1916.

The average strength of the Battalion during August 1916 was:- 25 Officers & 946 Other Ranks

2 Officers & 33 Other Ranks were admitted to Hospital during this period of which 8 Other Ranks rejoined the Battalion and 27 Other Ranks were evacuated out of the Divisional Area

31/8/16

G. Rennie Lt. Col
Comdg 7 K.R.Rifles

Instructions regarding War Diaries and Intelligence Summaries are contained in F. S. Regs., Part II. and the Staff Manual respectively. Title Pages will be prepared in manuscript.

WAR DIARY
or
INTELLIGENCE SUMMARY

(Erase heading not required.)

Army Form C. 2118.

1.

Place	Date	Hour	Summary of Events and Information	Remarks and references to Appendices
GESAINCOURT	Aug 1st		Batt [illegible] [illegible] GESAINCOURT [illegible] [illegible] CAPT H.H. [illegible] [illegible] wounded	[illegible]
	Aug 2nd		Bn training	
	Aug 3rd		Lt J.N. MARTIN reported for [illegible] Bn Training [illegible]	
	Aug 4–5th		Bn training	[illegible]
	Aug 6		Transport started by road for BERNANCOURT [illegible] FAIRIE [illegible] through [illegible]	[illegible]
	Aug 7.		Bn marched to CANDAS [illegible] in a field for [illegible] and then entrained.	[illegible]
BERNANCOURT	Aug 8		Bn detrained at [illegible] and marched [illegible]	[illegible]
	Aug 9		Lt A.B. BERNARD, [illegible] STEWART, J.H. TURNER [illegible] to 16th K.R.R. Bn [illegible]	[illegible]
	Aug 10		C.O. & Coy Commanders reconnoitred the German 2nd line	
RESERVE	Aug 11th		Bn relieved N. Yorkshire [illegible] in [illegible] trench	[illegible]
SUPPORT	Aug 12th		Bn relieved E. Yorkshire Regt in the German support line. 2Lt C.A. MEGAVIN [illegible] to England [illegible]	[illegible]
	Aug 13th		"A" Coy relieved part of [illegible] R.B. & 221 in [illegible] front line [illegible] in DELVILLE WOOD. [illegible] opposite ORCHARD TRENCH [illegible] to taking ORCHARD TRENCH. C.O. & all Coy Commanders reconnoitred same trench. 221 on our right, RB on our left. [illegible] of [illegible] stopped in GERMAN 2nd line & on the night 13–14th dug the following new trenches – [illegible] yds traversed trench connecting PEAR ST and ridge S11 c 8 3 facing N & E. – [illegible] yds trench in front of existing firing line opposite ORCHARD Trench – [illegible] yds trench connecting [illegible] 4th [illegible] in DELVILLE wood [illegible]	[illegible] Capt

2449 Wt. W14957/M90 750,000 1/16 J.B.C. & A. Forms/C.2118/12.

Instructions regarding War Diaries and Intelligence Summaries are contained in F. S. Regs., Part II. and the Staff Manual respectively. Title Pages will be prepared in manuscript.

WAR DIARY
or
INTELLIGENCE SUMMARY
(Erase heading not required.)

Army Form C. 2118.

Vol 16

2.

Place	Date	Hour	Summary of Events and Information	Remarks and references to Appendices
			deepened 170 yds of CT from GEORGE ST to PONT ST. 1 OR. wounded	
RESERVE.	Aug 14		Bn relieved in the morning by 8th KRR. & proceeded to POMMIERS TRENCH. 2Lt F.J. St Aubyn and 1 OR. wounded. Major J. Wormald posted to 2nd Bn K.R.R.	H a de V? Capt
	Aug 15 / 16		Resting in Reserve	H a de V? Capt H a de V? Capt
	Aug 17		Relieved 8th KRR in trenches facing ORCHARD Trench immediately N of DELVILLE WOOD. 2Lt A.L. MACKENZIE wounded 1 OR killed 3 OR wounded. Heavy bombardment by our artillery during relief	
	Aug 18th		Bn was ordered to attack German ORCHARD Trench preceded by a heavy bombardment. C & D Coys under 2Lt WHITLEY & CAPT BLAND were the assaulting Coys in two waves. B Coy under Capt BARTHOLOMEW in support, A Coy under 2Lt ROMER in reserve. At 6am our artillery bombardment commenced and continued according to programme till Zero 2.45pm when intense Field Artillery bombarded Enemy front line trench. Some casualties were caused by our own artillery preparation including 2Lt WHITLEY who nevertheless remained at his post. At Zero, the two leading waves left their trenches at 50 yds interval & advanced close up & even into our own barrage. Immediately the barrage lifted, ORCHARD Trench was occupied. It was found much damaged & only a few unwounded Germans ~~prisoners~~ who did not survive. There were many Germans buried. On the barrage lifting still further, the leading wave again advanced over the open for about 100 yds, the right flank being thrown back on to the FLERS ROAD; the left flank being found to be also in the air, was thrown back as well in order to join up	H a de V? Capt H a de V? Capt

2449 Wt. W14957/M90 750,000 1/16 J.B.C. & A. Forms/C.2118/12.

Army Form C. 2118.

Instructions regarding War Diaries and Intelligence Summaries are contained in F. S. Regs., Part II. and the Staff Manual respectively. Title Pages will be prepared in manuscript.

WAR DIARY
or
INTELLIGENCE SUMMARY
(Erase heading not required.)

Place	Date	Hour	Summary of Events and Information	Remarks and references to Appendices
			with the Coy of the 7th RB who were consolidating in ORCHARD TRENCH on our right, which they had captured. The 2nd wave quickly joined the leading wave & the process of consolidation [illegible] by groups of men digging themselves in. Shortly after 3 platoons of the supporting Coy reinforced and assisted in the consolidation, the remaining platoon stopping in ORCHARD Trench in support. These posts were linked up during the night forming one continuous line. During the whole time of consolidation a considerable M.G. and rifle fire at close range from a Strong Point in the N.E. corner of [illegible] WOOD caused many casualties, but was kept down to a certain extent by R. [illegible] under Lt FARMER in bombing efforts [illegible] killed & [illegible] Fumite bombs & rifle grenades were used with good effect. It had been promised that this Strong Point would be heavily bombarded for 2 hours prior [to] Zero, but only an occasional shell fell in this neighbourhood. A Coy carried material the remainder of the day & all night to the four Companies. One Coy from the 8th R.B. was called upon & dug a Communication Trench from our original front line to ORCHARD Trench. [illegible] and RE made two Strong Points, one on the right within 20 yds of [illegible] ORCHARD Trench, and one 20 yds in front of ORCHARD Trench [illegible] a 3rd being made near the junction of [illegible] & ORCHARD [illegible]	[illegible]

2449 Wt. W14957/M90 750,000 1/16 J.B.C. & A. Forms/C.2118/12.

Army Form C. 2118.

WAR DIARY
or
INTELLIGENCE SUMMARY
(Erase heading not required.)

4. Vol 16

Instructions regarding War Diaries and Intelligence Summaries are contained in F. S. Regs., Part II. and the Staff Manual respectively. Title Pages will be prepared in manuscript.

Place	Date	Hour	Summary of Events and Information	Remarks and references to Appendices
			The 43rd IB cooperated on our right by attacking a portion of DELVILLE WOOD but leaving a gap of about 400 yds on our right. The 7th RB cooperated on our left. Their Right Coy consolidating in ORCHARD Trench and 30 yds of WOOD LANE, their Left Coy having been wiped out, and the attack by the Bde on the left having failed to reach its objective. All ranks behaved magnificently	HAWDT
			Casualties. Killed Lt CEG FARMER, Lt HON. BD. BUTLER. Wounded Lt J.N. MARTIN 2Lt C. WHITLEY, 2Lt C.H. DAVIDSON, 2Lt S.T. BIRD (died of wounds 20/8/16)	
			O.R. Killed 42. Wounded 174, missing 4.	
	Aug 19th		Day was quiet till 8pm except for very accurate sniping from DELVILLE WOOD. At 8pm the enemy opened a heavy bombardment on our trenches and a barrage behind, after which the enemy made a feeble counter attack which was easily driven off. After everything had quieted down, the bn was relieved by the 2nd Worcesters ~~8 KRR~~ & proceeded to POMMIERS TRENCH	HAWDT Capt
			Casualties O.R. Killed 9. Wounded 25, Missing 1.	
POMMIERS	Aug 20–24		Resting at POMMIERS	HAWDT Capt
	Aug 22		1 O.R. Wounded	
	Aug 23		Draft of 90 O.R. joined	HAWDT Capt
	Aug 24		Bn relieved 8th KRR in HOP ALLEY at night. There was considerable hostile shell fire & sniping. Casualties O.R. 1 Killed, 11 wounded	HAWDT Capt

2449 Wt. W14957/M90 750,000 1/16 J.B.C. & A. Forms/C.2118/12.

Instructions regarding War Diaries and Intelligence Summaries are contained in F. S. Regs., Part II. and the Staff Manual respectively. Title Pages will be prepared in manuscript.

WAR DIARY
or
INTELLIGENCE SUMMARY
(Erase heading not required.)

Army Form C. 2118.

5

Vol 16

Place	Date	Hour	Summary of Events and Information	Remarks and references to Appendices
H.Q. ALLE[illegible]			The condition of the trenches was very bad, & many dead lying in and about the trench. On our right the 7 R.B. on our left 7 K.R.R. who were relieved that night by the 9 R.B	H.de[illegible]
	Aug 25		Intermittent hostile shelling & sniping. About 8 pm we started a heavy bombardment some way to the South, which gradually spread Northward. The enemy appeared nervous & opened a heavy bombardment on our trenches. The D.L.I. (43 [illegible]) relieved the 9 [illegible] ([illegible]) Killed CAPT G.H. [illegible] O.R. 10 Killed 15 wounded	
	Aug 26		Intermittent shelling during the day. Our own artillery bombarded [illegible] & caused casualties 1 O.R. Killed 4 O.R. wounded. [illegible] relieved [illegible] by the 1st R.W. Fusiliers & proceeded to DERNANCOURT. A Draft of 52 O.R. joined	H.de [illegible]
	Aug 28		Training of draft & inspection of remainder.	H.de [illegible]
	Aug 29		B.G.C. inspected 2 latest drafts. Draft of 15 O.R. joined ([illegible])	H.de [illegible]
	Aug 30		Bn moved by train at short notice from ALBERT [illegible] arriving at ABBEVILLE in the evening & marching to billets at [illegible] ~~[illegible]~~. ~~[illegible]~~ Transport went by road	H.de [illegible]
	Aug 31		Transport arrived 4 pm	H.de [illegible]

Confidential.

7th (Service) Battalion

The King's Royal Rifle Corps.

War Diary

From 1st to 30th September 1916

Volume 17.

Army Form C. 2118.

Instructions regarding War Diaries and Intelligence Summaries are contained in F. S. Regs., Part II. and the Staff Manual respectively. Title Pages will be prepared in manuscript.

WAR DIARY
or
INTELLIGENCE SUMMARY

(Erase heading not required.)

Place	Date	Hour	Summary of Events and Information	Remarks and references to Appendices
~~[illegible]~~ METTIGNY	Sept 1		[illegible]	[illegible]
	2			
	3		[illegible]	[illegible]
	4		[illegible]	[illegible]
	5		[illegible]	[illegible]
	6		[illegible]	
	7		[illegible]	
	8		[illegible]	
	9		[illegible] Major R. Paget [illegible] Lt ~~[illegible]~~ [illegible] to England, wounded	
	10		Bn left METTIGNY at [illegible] by [illegible]	[illegible]

2449 Wt. W14957/M90 750,000 1/16 J.B.C. & A. Forms/C.2118/12.

Army Form C. 2118.

Vol 14

Page 2

Instructions regarding War Diaries and Intelligence Summaries are contained in F. S. Regs., Part II. and the Staff Manual respectively. Title pages will be prepared in manuscript.

WAR DIARY
or
INTELLIGENCE SUMMARY.
(Erase heading not required.)

Place	Date	Hour	Summary of Events and Information	Remarks and references to Appendices
DERNANCOURT	Sept 10		DERNANCOURT 6pm & going into billets. Movement arrangements were excellent and all officers had seats in cars – a great contrast to the down journey in wet supply trucks	[illegible] Major
FRICOURT	11th		Bn marched to tents at FRICOURT CAMP	[illegible] Major
MONTAUBAN	12th		Bn moved into Reserve trenches in MONTAUBAN ALLEY. 2Lt E.S. BLACKBOURNE joined Bn	[illegible] Major
	13th		MONTAUBAN ALLEY. Lt BOOTHROYD to England sick	[illegible] Major
	14th		At 11.45pm Bn moved up to DELVILLE WOOD & took up its position in artillery formation in the front of the wood at 1am. Details & 1st Line Transport moved forward to MONTAUBAN 2Lt G.L. SPRECKLEY joined Bn.	[illegible] Major

1577 Wt. W10791/1773 500,000 1/15 D. D. & L. A.D.S.S./Forms/C. 2118.

Instructions regarding War Diaries and Intelligence Summaries are contained in F. S. Regs., Part II. and the Staff Manual respectively. Title Pages will be prepared in manuscript.

WAR DIARY
or
INTELLIGENCE SUMMARY
(Erase heading not required.)

Army Form C. 2118.

Place	Date	Hour	Summary of Events and Information	Remarks and references to Appendices
Front Line [illegible]			[illegible] [illegible] ~~[illegible]~~ (the assembly trenches) near the front [illegible] of [illegible], 7th RB on the right, 41st [illegible] on the left. [illegible] [illegible] the 8th KRR + 7th + 8th RB in the [illegible] left [illegible] trenches just in front of [illegible] WOOD – Brown [illegible] + GREEN [illegible] [illegible] [illegible] [illegible] [illegible] [illegible] [illegible] stop [illegible] but [illegible] [illegible] [illegible] at the ~~[illegible]~~ SWITCH TRENCH [illegible] [illegible] [illegible] [illegible] the 7th KRR + 7th RB passed through them and [illegible] occupied the GAP trench + proceeded to [illegible]. Tanks which were used for the first time, came up on the right flank. After a short time the Tanks [illegible] and the 42nd IB passed through us, but were unable to take their objective owing to M.G. fire from the flanks. FLERS on the left flank was not occupied till the afternoon. There was some confusion in the trenches owing to [illegible] of the 42nd IB coming back into our line and many of the 7th RB going forward with the 42nd IB. Heavy shelling continued all day. At dusk	

2449 Wt. W14957/M90 750,000 1/16 J.B.C. & A. Forms/C.2118/12.

Instructions regarding War Diaries and Intelligence Summaries are contained in F. S. Regs., Part II. and the Staff Manual respectively. Title Pages will be prepared in manuscript.

WAR DIARY
or
INTELLIGENCE SUMMARY
(Erase heading not required.)

Army Form C. 2118.

Vol 17
Page 4

Place	Date	Hour	Summary of Events and Information	Remarks and references to Appendices
	Sept 16th		The 43rd I.B. relieved the 42nd I.B. and 7th KRR & 7th RB who occupied GREEN & BROWN STREETS E. of DELVILLE WOOD where they remained untill the following evening being shelled the whole time. At 7 pm orders were received to retire to the transport Camp at FRICOURT with permission to bivouac on the way.	
			Casualties for two days 12 officers and the Medical Officer. O.R. Killed 21; Wounded 189, missing 120. Great gallantry was shown by all ranks	
			The following officers were wounded Major R. PAGET, CAPT. E.C. BLAND CAPT F.G. de SATGÉ, 2Lts MLR. ROMER, RWV. MIDLANE, N.W. PALMER, H.S. BREWSTER. J.E.G. LAMB, G.H. EDWARDS, E.S. BLACKBOURNE, G.L. SPRECKLEY CAPT & ADJT M.J. ST AUBYN, CAPT W. MORRISON RAMC.	H.W.S.[?]
			Draft of 16 O.R. joined the bn	
DERNANCOURT	17th		3 pm bn marched to DERNANCOURT & billeted	
"	18th		2Lts FEXRARD and ELLESMOOR & 40R joined bn. Lt BREWSTER to England wounded	
"	19th		Address by Bt Gen SKINNER comdg 41st IB	H.W.S.[?]

2449 Wt. W14957/M90 750,000 1/16 J.B.C. & A. Forms/C.2118/12.

Instructions regarding War Diaries and Intelligence Summaries are contained in F. S. Regs., Part II. and the Staff Manual respectively. Title Pages will be prepared in manuscript.

WAR DIARY
or
INTELLIGENCE SUMMARY
(Erase heading not required.)

Army Form C. 2118.

Place	Date	Hour	Summary of Events and Information	Remarks and references to Appendices
~~Sept~~ 2				
[illegible]COURT	Sept 19		Lt LAMB [illegible] Lt [illegible]	[illegible]
	Sept 20		Capt F. C. BLAKE [illegible] Lt ROMER	[illegible]
	Sept 21		Transport [illegible] to [illegible]	
	Sept 22		Bn [illegible] by bus [illegible]	[illegible]
LISIEUX	Sept 23			
	24			
	25			
	26		Transport left [illegible] by [illegible] to [illegible]	[illegible]
[illegible]	27		Bn relieved [illegible] Queens [illegible] by day in [illegible] sector.	[illegible]
	29		Quiet day	[illegible]
	30		Quiet day [illegible]	[illegible]

[illegible signature]

2449 Wt. W14957/M90 750,000 1/16 J.B.C. & A. Forms/C.2118/12.

7th (S) Bn King's Royal Rifle Corps

Septr 1916

The average strength of the Battalion during Septr 1916 was –

17 Officers & 840 Other Ranks.

1 Officer & 324 Other Ranks were admitted to Hospital during this period of which 5 Other Ranks rejoined the Battalion & 1 Officer Invalided to England & 6 Other Ranks were evacuated out of the Divisional Area

G. Rennie Lt-Col
Comdg 7th K.R. Rifles

30/9/16

Vol 17

[illegible] Battalion

[illegible] Corps

War Diary:

[illegible] 1st to 31st October 1916

— Volume 18 —

Instructions regarding War Diaries and Intelligence Summaries are contained in F. S. Regs., Part II. and the Staff Manual respectively. Title Pages will be prepared in manuscript.

WAR DIARY or ~~INTELLIGENCE SUMMARY~~

(Erase heading not required.)

VOL 18

Army Form C. 2118.

Place	Date	Hour	Summary of Events and Information	Remarks and references to Appendices
F.2 Sector	2 Oct. 1916		2 Lieut C.E. PULLINGER joined Bat. for duty. 1.O.R. wounded.	GR
"	5.10.16		Lieut P.K. HAWORTH rejoined Bat for duty, the following from the Sussex Regt also joined for duty	GR
			2nd Lt S. WIGGINS, 2Lt J.E.M. MACGREGOR, 2Lt G.B. MOUNTFORD.	GR
"	8.10.16		2Lt P.F. WALFORD joined Bat. 3. O.R. wounded.	GR
"	9.10.16		Major P.A.W. LAYE joined the Bat.	GR
"	10.10.16		2. O.R. wounded.	GR
"	12.10.16		2Lt C. WHITLEY rejoined the Bat.	GR
RIVIERA	15.10.16		Bat. went into Bgd Reserve in billets in RIVIERA. 2. OR. wounded.	GR
"	16.10.16		2. O.R. wounded.	GR
"	18.10.16		1. O.R. wounded.	GR
"	19.10.16		2nd Lt H.S. COOK joined the Bat.	GR
F.3 Sector	21.10.16		Took over F.3 Sector. 7th R.B on our right. 42 Bgde on our left.	GR
"	23.10.16		4. O.R. accidently wounded.	GR
BEAUMETZ	25.10.16		The Bat. moved to BEAUMETZ on the Div being relieved by the 12th Div.	GR
SOMBRIN	26.10.16		The Bat. marched to SOMBRIN for rest & training.	GR
"	31.10.16		Training continued under bad conditions	GR

G. Rennie Lt Col
Cmdg 7. KRRifles

2449 Wt. W14957/M90 750,000 1/16 J.B.C. & A. Forms/C.2118/12.

7th (Service) Bn King's Royal Rifles

October 1916

The average strength of the Battalion during October 1916, has been

20 Officers 687 Other Ranks.

During the month One Officer & 52 Other Ranks have been admitted to hospital, the officer & 18 O.R. rejoined the Bn during the month and 17 O.R. were evacuated out of the Divisional Area.

G. Rennie
Lt Col
Comdg 7th K.R. Rifles

31/10/16

Secret

Vol 18

7th (Service) Battalion

The King's Royal Rifle Corps.

War Diary

From 1st to 30th November, 1916

Volume 19

Instructions regarding War Diaries and Intelligence Summaries are contained in F. S. Regs., Part II. and the Staff Manual respectively. Title pages will be prepared in manuscript.

WAR DIARY

~~or~~

~~INTELLIGENCE~~ SUMMARY.

(*Erase heading not required.*)

Army Form C. 2118.

Volume 19

NOVEMBER 1916.

Place	Date	Hour	Summary of Events and Information	Remarks and references to Appendices
SOMBRIN	NOV		Change in Establishment – Reduction of 24 Private Riflemen [illegible] in Establishment of a H.Q. Coy [illegible]	
	1		Training continued under fairly good conditions. 2nd Lieut [illegible] [illegible] Bn from [illegible] [illegible]	
	2		Draft of 32 O.R. joined Battalion	[illegible]
	[illegible]		Draft of 4 O.R. joined Battalion	[illegible]
	7		Draft of 37 O.R. joined Battalion	[illegible]
	19		[illegible]	[illegible]
	21		2nd Lieut [illegible] JACKMAN [illegible] posted [illegible]	
	23		[illegible] RICCARD [illegible]	[illegible]
	24		[illegible] battalion [illegible] Rance [illegible]	
			Lt Colonel C.B.J. RICCARD [illegible] of the battalion	
	26		[illegible] ST AUBYN [illegible] battalion [illegible]	[illegible]
	30		[illegible]	[illegible]
			Battalion [illegible] at SOMBRIN [illegible]	

C.B.J. Riccard Lt Col
Comdg [illegible]

[illegible]/1916

A5834 Wt W4273/M687 750,000 8/16 D. D. & L. Ltd. Forms/C.2118/13.

7th (S) Bn King's Royal Rifles

November 1916

The average strength of the Battalion during November 1916, has been :-

22 Officers 811 Other Ranks

During the month one Officer and 68 Other Ranks have been admitted to hospital, 28 other Ranks rejoined the Bn, & the Officer and 32 other Ranks were evacuated out of the Divisional Area.

30/11/16

C.B. Riccard Lt-Col
Comdg 7th K.R. Rifles.

Secret

Vol 19

7th (Service) Battalion,
The King's Royal Rifle Corps.

War Diary
From 1st December 1916
To 31st December 1916

Volume
~~20~~

Army Form C. 2118.

WAR DIARY

~~or~~

~~INTELLIGENCE SUMMARY.~~

(Erase heading not required.)

Instructions regarding War Diaries and Intelligence Summaries are contained in F. S. Regs., Part II. and the Staff Manual respectively. Title pages will be prepared in manuscript.

DECEMBER 1916. VOLUME 20.

Place	Date	Hour	Summary of Events and Information	Remarks and references to Appendices
SOMBRIN	Dec. 1st		The Battalion continued training.	M.J.S.A.
	" 2nd		Major E. H. HANKS } Captain R. C. PROCTER } 2/17th London Regt. joined Battalion.	M.J.S.A.
			2/Lieut F. R. WILLIAMS joined Battalion	M.J.S.A.
	" 8th		Captain E. FAIRLIE rejoined Battalion from wounds	
	" 9th		Major C. K. HOWARD-BURY joined Battalion. Lt. Col. C. B. J. RICCARD 2/6th Essex Regt. relinquished temporary command of Battalion. Draft of 46 O.R. joined	M.J.S.A. M.J.S.A.
	" 10th		Major C. K. HOWARD-BURY assumed temporary command of the Battalion	M.J.S.A.
	" 12th		Draft of 46 O.R. joined.	
	" 14th		Draft of Lieut. B. H. SUMNER and 75 O.R. joined	M.J.S.A.
	" 15th		1 O.R. accidentally wounded.	
BEAUMETZ	" 17th		The Battalion moved into Divisional Reserve at BEAUMETZ. Training continued.	M.J.S.A.
F1 sector	" 22nd		The Battalion took over trenches from the 8th K.R.R.C. The 7th R.B. were on the left and the 30th Div. on the right	M.J.S.A.
			1 O.R. killed 2 O.R. wounded, by shell fire at BEAUMETZ, when 80 men had been left for a class of instruction	
	"24th		1 O.R. killed. 1 O.R. wounded and to duty.	M.J.S.A.
RIVIERE	" 28th		The Battalion moved into Brigade Reserve at RIVIERE every man being employed on working parties, mending the trenches. The weather was very bad, snow & rain then a frost followed by a thaw with more rain, so that the fire trenches & communication trenches fell in everywhere & the resulting state of the trenches was deplorable. As gas was suspected in the German trenches, an organized bombardment was carried out by the heavies on Dec 27th & 28th with good results.	M.J.S.A.

C K Bury Major
Cmdg 7th K.R.Rifles.

A5834 Wt. W4973/M687 750,000 8/16 D. D. & L. Ltd. Forms/C.2118/13.

7th (Service) Bn King's Royal Rifles

December 1916

The average strength of the Battalion during October 1916, has been

28 Officers 955 Other Ranks.

During the month 63 Other Ranks have been admitted to Hospital, of which 7 have been evacuated from the Divisional Area & 36 have rejoined the Bn.

31/12/16

C H [illegible] Major
Comdg 7th K. R. Rifles

Vol 20

Secret

7th (Service) Bn

King's Royal Rifle Corps

War Diary

From 1st to 31st

January 1917

Volume 21

Instructions regarding War Diaries and Intelligence Summaries are contained in F. S. Regs., Part II. and the Staff Manual respectively. Title pages will be prepared in manuscript.

WAR DIARY ~~or~~ ~~INTELLIGENCE SUMMARY.~~

(Erase heading not required.)

JANUARY 1917.

VOLUME 21

Army Form C. 2118.

Place	Date	Hour	Summary of Events and Information	Remarks and references to Appendices
RIVIERE	JAN 1st		In BRIGADE RESERVE	Pau
"	2nd		2nd LIEUTS A.F.R. WYSE, C.M. SIMPSON, R.B. ROBINSON, S. PARK joined battalion & are 7th SEAFORTH HIGHLDRS. 10th A & S HIGHLDRS temporarily attached.	Pau
			Draft of 18 O.R. joined battalion.	
F SECTOR	3rd		Battalion returned into the trenches in F SECTOR. The 7th RB were on the left & the 30th DIV on the right.	Pau
"	4th		Situation quiet. 2nd LIEUT K.W. McWILLIAMSON joined battalion for duty.	Pau
"	5th		2nd LIEUT H.S. COOK invalided to ENGLAND. 2 O.R. wounded including one at duty.	Pau
"	6th		Situation quiet.	Pau
"	7th		Left Coy reports increased activity on part of enemy but centre Coy reports exceptionally quiet. Many grenades fell in enemy's own wire opposite 17.10.	Pau
"	8th		Enemy's trenches appear to be in a bad state about R29 C7.0. to R29 C9.4. Enemy's working party at R29 D15 dispersed by L.G. Enemy continue to show usual activity. There was a loud explosion heard in enemy's trench at R29 C04. Suggests grenades exploding.	Pau
	8th		Decreased activity on part of enemy. Searchlight played for a few minutes opposite F174. Two enemy aeroplanes which came over our line were driven off by our A.A. at 2.15 pm. 1 O.R. killed.	
"	9th		The battalion was relieved by the 8th KRRC. Relief all correct. The battalion moved back to BEAUMETZ, into Divisional Reserve.	Pau
BEAUMETZ	10th		2nd LIEUT L.A. BLACKETT joined battalion for duty.	Pau
"	11th		Battalion moved into billets at SIMENCOURT, owing to heavy shelling of BEAUMETZ by enemy artillery.	Pau
SIMENCOURT	12th		Battalion cleaning up.	Pau
"	13th		Battalion finding working parties for hutting & bunking under R.E. & Corps troops.	Pau

A5834 Wt. W4973/M687 750,000 8/16 D. D. & L. Ltd. Forms C.2118/13.

Instructions regarding War Diaries and Intelligence Summaries are contained in F. S. Regs., Part II. and the Staff Manual respectively. Title pages will be prepared in manuscript.

WAR DIARY

or

~~INTELLIGENCE SUMMARY.~~

(*Erase heading not required.*)

Jan 1917

Army Form C. 2118.

Place	Date	Hour	Summary of Events and Information	Remarks and references to Appendices
SIMENCOURT	JAN 14th		Battalion continues to find working parties as before.	[illegible]
"	JAN 15th		Battalion relieves 8th K.R.R.C. in the trenches in F SECTOR. Relief correct. On our left 7th R.B. on our right 49th DIV.	[illegible]
F SECTOR.	16th		MAJOR H.M.B. DE SALES LATERRIERE to staff of Third Army School 16.1.17. & is struck off the battalion strength.	[illegible]
"	17th		Situation quiet.	[illegible]
"	18th		At 1.40 am enemy searchlight active 600 yds W of FICHEUX MILL. At 11.40 pm our STOKES MORTAR fired 20 rounds on enemy machine gun at R 29 C 65.15 & silenced it. Enemy M.G. judged by rate of fire to be an automatic rifle of new type traversed parapet of right Coy. Position R 35 A 46. It was silenced by our T.M's.	[illegible]
"	19th		No enemy patrolling activity. All indications point to enemy front line being lightly held. Enemy sentry at Z 18 heard whistling the "Spring Song" at 12 mn!	[illegible]
"	20th		Enemy appear to be working hard on their front & support lines, & wire.	
"	21st		Battalion relieved by 8th KRRC. Relief correct. Battalion returned to RIVIERE.	[illegible]
RIVIERE	22nd		2nd LIEUT L.R. THOMAS joined battalion for duty. Draft of 18 O.R. joined.	[illegible]
"	23rd		Battalion in BRIGADE RESERVE finding working parties.	[illegible]
"	25th		2nd LIEUT J.A. JOHNSTON SCOTTISH RIFLES joined battalion for duty.	[illegible]
"	26th		2nd LIEUT R.C. STEARNS joined battalion for duty.	[illegible]
"	27th		Battalion relieved 8th KRRC in F SECTOR. Relief correct. On our left 7th RB on our right 5th YORKS & LANCS.	[illegible]
F SECTOR	28th		Our Field Guns fired on German front line & support in cooperation with an aeroplane which was flying low to take photographs. At 3.30 pm enemy T.M. & some bombs active on left Coy searching for T.M. emplacements. Several direct hits on support line between FLOOD ST & FRENCH ST.	[illegible]
"	29th		At 2.35 pm hostile aeroplane driven back by our A.A. & M.G. [illegible]	[illegible]
	30th		Enemy trench mortars active on our left Coy front line. No particular damage done.	[illegible]

Army Form C. 2118.

Instructions regarding War Diaries and Intelligence Summaries are contained in F. S. Regs., Part II. and the Staff Manual respectively. Title pages will be prepared in manuscript.

WAR DIARY
or
INTELLIGENCE SUMMARY.
(Erase heading not required.)

Place	Date	Hour	Summary of Events and Information	Remarks and references to Appendices
I SECTOR	JAN 30		Casualties from enemy [illegible] fire in our front line: 2 OR wounded [illegible] duty.	[illegible]
"	JAN 31		Situation quiet. Very [illegible]	[illegible]
			2nd Lieuts R.B. MOUNTFORD, [illegible] HAWES, J.E. HARGREAVES [illegible] attached to 1st Bn not transferred to Battalion [illegible] effect from [illegible] 24 O.R. have been transferred to King's [illegible] from 24. 2. [illegible] 27. 1. 16.	

31/1 1917

[illegible]
Comdg. 1st [illegible]
King's Royal Rifle Corps

A5834 Wt. W4973/M687 750,000 8/16 D. D. & L. Ltd. Forms C.2118/13.

7th (S) Bn. King's Royal Rifle Corps

January 1917

The average strength of the Battalion during January 1917 has been

34 Officers 1002 Other Ranks

During the month 4 Officers and 23 other ranks have been admitted to hospital, one officer & 7 other ranks rejoined the Bn during the month and 9 other ranks were evacuated out of the Divisional Area

31/1/17

[illegible] Lt-Col
Comdg 7th K.R.Rifles

Secret

WO 95/1921

7th (Service) Battalion,

The King's Royal Rifle Corps

WAR DIARY

From 1st to 28th February 1917

Volume 22

Instructions regarding War Diaries and Intelligence Summaries are contained in F. S. Regs., Part II. and the Staff Manual respectively. Title pages will be prepared in manuscript.

WAR DIARY

or

~~INTELLIGENCE SUMMARY.~~

FEBRUARY 1917 (Erase heading not required.)

Army Form C. 2118.

VOL. 22

Place	Date	Hour	Summary of Events and Information	Remarks and references to Appendices
F2 SECTOR	Feb 1st 1917		A few 77 mm & about 30 4.2 dropped about head of FORREST ST & FIDDLE ST. One or two shells gave out peculiar blueish green smoke which hung about for some minutes. One direct hit on 2" T.M. emplacement & one on FORREST ST. doing considerable damage. Markings of nose cap found 330 G(?) 2 140 T 15	Paul
			830 pm. singing opposite left company & a voice called out "When are you coming over Tommy".	
			645 pm Working party heard & interrupted by our L.G.s.	
			1130 pm Sound of mining reported by 2" Mortars under their dug-outs in FORREST ST.	
	Feb 2nd	9-10am	10 4.2 & about 60 77 mm on support & centre coy. chiefly about FORREST ST. Majority fell in wire 2 direct hits on issue of NAMELESS SAP & trench doing some damage.	Paul
SIMENCOURT		3.40am	Fired at our working party from R 35 A 20.85 without doing any damage.	
			Relieved by 1/4th WEST RIDING REGT in F2 SECTOR. 3 O.R. wounded. Bn marched to SIMENCOURT.	
	Feb 3rd		Bn marched from SIMENCOURT to billets at SOMBRIN.	Paul
SOMBRIN	Feb 4th		Bn finds working parties at MONDICOURT, LUCHEUX, IVERGNY, LE SOUICH. Bn HQ SOMBRIN	Paul
"	Feb 6th		2nd LIEUTS C.M. SIMPSON, S.G. ROBINSON, & S. PARK all 10th Argyll & Sutherland Hglrs & 2nd LIEUT. A.F.R. WYSE 7th Seaforth Hglrs who have been temporarily attached to the Bn rejoined their own units.	Paul
"	F[illegible] to 16th		Working party numbers were reduced which enabled Bn to have one coy for training at SOMBRIN.	Paul
"	Feb 16th		CAPT B.H. WILLIAMSON rejoined Bn from ENGLAND (sickness).	Paul
			Draft of one CSM, 4 Sgts, 14 OR. joined Bn.	
"	Feb 20th		2nd LIEUT [illegible] W. BORTHWICK joined Bn for duty.	Paul
"	Feb 21st		2nd LIEUTS W.D. DRING, G.A. CARR joined Bn on first appointment.	Paul
			2nd LIEUT J.P. ELLSMOOR admitted to F.A.	

1577 Wt. W10791/1773 500,000 1/15 D. D. & L. A.D.S.S./Forms/C. 2118.

Army Form C. 2118.

Instructions regarding War Diaries and Intelligence Summaries are contained in F. S. Regs., Part II. and the Staff Manual respectively. Title pages will be prepared in manuscript.

WAR DIARY
or
INTELLIGENCE SUMMARY.

FEBRUARY 1917 (Contd) *(Erase heading not required.)* Vol 22 [illegible]

Place	Date	Hour	Summary of Events and Information	Remarks and references to Appendices
POUBRIN [illegible]	Feb 25th		Bn. Staff riding [illegible] HAUDICOURT. Bn HQ [illegible] 2 days. 2nd LIEUT J.W. BLAKE transferred on probation to RFC [illegible]	[illegible]
"	Feb 26th		2nd LIEUT C.R. TOBITT proceeded to ENGLAND for Course [illegible] Engineering [illegible] CHATHAM.	[illegible]
			Weather during month for first twenty days cold [illegible] Food & liquids frozen [illegible] was [illegible] in several [illegible] of the trenches during the first two days of the month was good. The thaw began on the 20th which continued [illegible] [illegible] roads [illegible] [illegible] fairly good. Adequate accommodation for the troops.	

C.W. Bury [illegible] Lt Col
Comdg 7th (Service) Bn
King's Royal Rifle Corps

1577 Wt. W10791/1773 500,000 1/15 D. D. & L. A.D.S.S./Forms/C. 2118.

7th (S) Bn King's Royal Rifles

February 1917.

The average strength of the Battalion during February 1917 has been

35 Officers 999 Other Ranks

During the month 1 Officer and 60 other ranks have been admitted to hospital, 27 other ranks rejoined the Bn during the month 12 other ranks were evacuated out of Divisional area & 2 other ranks died in hospital

28/2/17

[signature] Lt Col
Comdg 7th (S) Bn
King's Royal Rifles

Vol 22

Secret

7th (Service) Battalion

The King's Royal Rifle Corps

War Diary

From 1st to 31st March 1917

Volume 23.

"Original"

Instructions regarding War Diaries and Intelligence Summaries are contained in F. S. Regs., Part II. and the Staff Manual respectively. Title pages will be prepared in manuscript.

WAR DIARY for MARCH 1917

~~INTELLIGENCE SUMMARY.~~

(Erase heading not required.)

Army Form C. 2118.

Volume 23.

Place	Date	Hour	Summary of Events and Information	Remarks and references to Appendices
SOMBRIN	1st – 15th		Batt. HQ in comfortable billets at SOMBRIN. The training of specialists was proceeded with, but no company training was possible as two companies were employed on railway construction at MONDICOURT and two at SAULTY on similar work. These parties only rejoined a day or two previous to the Battalion moving.	
			The severe frost of the previous month had broken but the weather continued cold and unfavourable. The thaw reduced all roads to a very bad state and no transport except the essential was allowed to move.	
			A company of the 9th Batt. was at SOMBRIN during part of this time, and the 9th Batt concert party gave several performances which were very much appreciated by our men.	M.J.S.A.
	1st		2/Lieut. C.R. TOBITT to R.E. course of instruction at CHATHAM and struck off strength	M.J.S.A.
	5th		2/Lieut. L.A. BLACKETT transferred to 2nd Battalion.	M.J.S.A.
SIMONCOURT	16th		The Battalion marched to SIMONCOURT and was accomodated in very draughty wooden huts. Transport and the Battalion BOAR moved to BERNEVILLE.	M.J.S.A.
	17th – 21st		Battalion training. Very little work was possible partly owing to bad weather, and partly because the Battalion was standing to for much of the time due to the German retirement south of ARRAS.	
	20th		On one of the two possible days for training on the prepared area, the battalion was confined to camp by the following message which is a good illustration of the care of our Staff in foreseeing every eventuality. "The Battalion will be clear of SIMONCOURT by 5 pm today, and will probably move to FOSSEUX or ARRAS."	
			The battalion remained at SIMONCOURT. FOSSEUX 4 miles WEST ← SIMONCOURT → ARRAS 8 miles EAST	
			Despite the efforts of the Town Major who, being a lawyer from London, was anxious to display agricultural knowledge about 30 year old pastures, a certain amount of football was possible, and an inter-platoon competition was started but could not be finished.	
	19th		Capt. E.C. BLAND rejoined from wounds.	M.J.S.A.
	21st		Lt. C.C. OMMANNEY joined on reposting. 2/Lieut P.F. WALFORD admitted to Field Ambulance with German measles.	M.J.S.A.

1577 Wt. W10791/1773 500,000 1/15 D. D. & L. A.D.S.S./Forms/C. 2118.

Instructions regarding War Diaries and Intelligence Summaries are contained in F. S. Regs., Part II. and the Staff Manual respectively. Title pages will be prepared in manuscript.

WAR DIARY
or
INTELLIGENCE SUMMARY.
(Erase heading not required.)

Army Form C. 2118.

Place	Date	Hour	Summary of Events and Information	Remarks and references to Appendices
ARRAS	22nd		The Battalion [illegible]	
	23rd		[illegible]	
BLUFF CAVE	24th – 28th		[illegible] HQ and [illegible] coy [illegible] connected [illegible] the original HQ [illegible]	
			1 O.R. [illegible]	
	25th		1 O.R. killed [illegible] wounded.	
	26th		2 O.R. wounded.	
			During these four days the battalion was finding working parties [illegible] part of the line.	
	28th		Battalion relieved 8th Battalion in trenches. Front line from M 11 B 3.2 to M 6 C 8.3 [illegible] 56th Div. on right, 7th R.B. on left. Two coys in front line [illegible] Two coys in reserve [illegible] Enemy holding TILLOY – [illegible] in front of [illegible]VILLE [illegible] Trenches mostly 800 – 1000 yards [illegible] rifle & M.G. fire [illegible] the forward coy HQ and Bn HQ being [illegible]	
	28th		2 O.R. wounded.	
	29th		2 O.R. killed, 3 O.R. wounded.	
	30th		2/Lieut. [illegible] rejoined [illegible]	
			[illegible] killed [illegible] O.R. wounded [illegible]	

1577 Wt. W10791/1773 500,[illegible] C. 2118.

8th King's Royal Rifle Corps

March 1917.

The average strength of the Battalion during March 1917 has been

36 Officers 974 Other Ranks

During the month 3 Officers and 44 other ranks have been admitted to hospital, 2 Officers & 19 other ranks rejoined the Battalion during the month & 14 other ranks were evacuated out of the Divisional Area

31/3/1917

C. W. Bury [?] Lt Col
Comdg 8 Bn
K R Rifles

Secret.

WO 95/1...

7th (Service) Battalion

The King's Royal Rifle Corps.

War Diary

From 1st to 30th April 1917.

Volume 24

Instructions regarding War Diaries and Intelligence Summaries are contained in F. S. Regs., Part II. and the Staff Manual respectively. Title pages will be prepared in manuscript.

WAR DIARY for APRIL 1917.

~~or~~

~~INTELLIGENCE SUMMARY.~~

(Erase heading not required.)

Army Form C. 2118.

Page 1

VOLUME 24

Place	Date	Hour	Summary of Events and Information	Remarks and references to Appendices
RONVILLE CAVES	1		Battalion was relieved in the line by 8th K.R.R.C. and moved to the Caves. HQ. in BLUFF, coys. in CHRIST CHURCH.	
			Lieut V. Taylor R.A.M.C. on rejoining from leave returned to a Field Ambulance and was replaced by Capt. T.A. Watson RAMC.	mJSA.
	2.		Lieut. F. J. St Aubyn rejoined from F.A. after an absence of more than two months.	
	3.		Lieut. W.W. Palmer rejoined from wounds. Batt. HQ. moved into Christchurch cave.	
DAINVILLE.	5.		The battalion moved to DAINVILLE.	
	7.		Capt. E. Fairlie appointed temp. 2nd in command of the 9th Batt.	
			During the first part of the above period the battalion found some working parties employed on digging assembly trenches.	M.JSA.
	5th		The Bombardment of the German lines began. There was an enormous concentration of Artillery all round ARRAS from 15" downwards and this bombardment went on unceasingly day & night.	WB
	8th		Easter Sunday. The bombardment of the German lines continued with increased violence. In the afternoon some large ammunition dumps in ACHICOURT were blown up. At 8 p.m the Battalion started to move up by platoons, through ACHICOURT to go into the caves at RONVILLE where the whole Brigade were to spend the night April 8th/9th. The move to the caves was accomplished without casualties though ACHICOURT had to be avoided owing to the constant explosions of shells from the dumps on fire. During the night all stores were issued & in the caves a wet but quiet night was spent. No sound of the concentrated bombardment overhead penetrated down to the depths below.	
	9th	7.30 A.M	The 7th K.R.R. & the 7th R.B. started out from the caves, each issuing by two exits & we made our way to the old British front line, which we occupied as the 41st Brigade was in Reserve while the 42nd & 43rd Brigade were taking part in the attack.	

Instructions regarding War Diaries and Intelligence Summaries are contained in F. S. Regs., Part II. and the Staff Manual respectively. Title pages will be prepared in manuscript.

WAR DIARY
or
INTELLIGENCE SUMMARY.
(Erase heading not required.)

Army Form C. 2118.

Place	Date	Hour	Summary of Events and Information	Remarks and references to Appendices
			There was a strong wind blowing with driving showers of rain – the trenches were occupied without trouble, though shortly afterwards we had three casualties in D.Coy from an unlucky shell. As the course of the battle progressed favourably, the Brigade were not required during the day. The Cavalry went through in the afternoon – but as the wire behind the further objective was uncut, their services could not be utilized. A very cold night was spent in the trenches with constant snow showers & by morning there was more than an inch of snow lying upon the ground.	[illegible]
	10th	10th	All through the 10th there were snow showers with occasional bright intervals. The order came that the Brigade was to move at 11am & the 7th K.O.R.L. were to move up to the BLUE LINE – the old German trenches in the	
	10th	11 AM	COJEUL Switch. This was accomplished without casualties & the amazing results of our shell fire on the German lines became apparent. The Bn was not left long here & after an hour's rest orders were received to move on & relieve the K.O.Y.L.I's who were supposed to be in the BROWN LINE in front of WANCOURT in N22a. Moving forward in Artillery formation up the Valley towards WANCOURT the Bn suddenly came under machine gun & rifle fire from the [illegible] from the direction of HILL 90 (N22c). Finding some newly discovered trenches in N15d, we occupied these until the ground had been reconnoitred in front. No signs of the K.O.Y.L.I. were to be found, but 150 yards in front, Germans were found holding the sunken road & many more appeared all along the crest of HILL 90. Under cover of a snowstorm A & D Companies under the command of Capt G H WILLIAMSON M.C.	

1577 Wt. W10791/1773 500,000 1/15 D. D. & L. A.D.S.S./Forms/C 2118.

Instructions regarding War Diaries and Intelligence Summaries are contained in F. S. Regs., Part II. and the Staff Manual respectively. Title pages will be prepared in manuscript.

WAR DIARY
or
INTELLIGENCE SUMMARY.

(Erase heading not required.)

Army Form C. 2118.

Page 3.

Place	Date	Hour	Summary of Events and Information	Remarks and references to Appendices
			pushed forward & reached the BROWN LINE in N16d. It was a very fine feat & would have been quite impossible except for the snowstorm which prevented much of the enfilade M.G. fire. They had however many casualties. 2nd Lt. F.R. WILLIAMS who was commanding D Coy was killed. Lient. F.J. ST AUBYN & 2nd Lt. P.F. WALFORD were also killed while LTS C. PULLINGER, S. WIGGINS, C.D. FERARD, J.G. JOHNSON & the younger WILLIAMSON were wounded & some 60 O.R's. were killed & wounded. About 20 Germans were captured & sent back, while a good many were killed.	CWB/41/01
			The K.O.Y.L.I's finding opposition in front had apparently moved up to the N. into another divisional front & were not where they were meant to be.	
			The position then on the evening of April 10th was that A & D. Coys were holding part of the BROWN LINE in N16d, while the other 2 Coys. were in support in N15d. We had captured a Machine Gun & a Trench Mortar here close to Bn. H.Q. The Germans were within 150 yds of the two support Coys. & there was no one on our right flank for 1300 yds. This being the case I asked for support on my right & the Brigadier sent up the 8th R.B. who prolonged my right flank towards the 56th Divn.	
			Battalion Headquarters was established in an old German Bomb Store full of bombs & trench mortar stores of all kinds, just in front of the support Coys.	
	11th	1AM	The night passed quite quietly. About 1A.M. the Brigadier came up & talked over the situation. He agreed that it was quite impossible to push on until Hill 90 had been taken by the 56th Divn. & that all we could do was to remain on the defensive. Any advance up the valley was sheer madness until the Machine Guns on HILL 90 which enfiladed the whole valley had been put out of action.	
	11th	4.30AM	The attached orders arrived & in spite of all protests we were ordered to carry them out. There was no time to copy them out & the originals had to be sent up to the forward Coys. B. & C. Companies supported by the 8th R.B. were to advance up the valley & to try & push on to WANCOURT. The 56th Division never left their trenches or made any attempt to take HILL 90.	Maps & Orders attached

Instructions regarding War Diaries and Intelligence Summaries are contained in F. S. Regs., Part II. and the Staff Manual respectively. Title pages will be prepared in manuscript.

WAR DIARY
or
INTELLIGENCE SUMMARY.
(Erase heading not required.)

Army Form C. 2118.

Place	Date	Hour	Summary of Events and Information	Remarks and references to Appendices
			B. Coy. under WHITLEY made a most gallant attempt to push forward but from the start it was an impossible task + the staff who had ordered [illegible] if they had ever come near enough to have looked at the ground would have [illegible] it too + would never have ordered the attack. WHITLEY was [illegible] that he was + his body was found nearest to the German wire which was [illegible] ment. The artillery preparation which [illegible] ordered [illegible] materialised – in fact the orders in many cases never arrived in time + the whole show was a complete failure from want of preparation + organisation on the part of the staff. The rest of the day was spent in our original positions + towards evening heavy snowstorms set in + before long there were two inches of snow on the ground. It was impossible to get in the wounded until after dark so that their sufferings were very much aggravated by the cold. That night we were relieved by the 8th K.R.R. + moved back to the old COJEUL SWITCH line, where a bitterly cold night was spent in the open, without any dugouts + [illegible] night.	[illegible]
	12th		The 12th was spent in these trenches + the 8th K.R.R. + [illegible] occupied WANCOURT without a casualty as HILL 90 had been evacuated during the night. The whole Division was relieved by the 50th DIVN + [illegible] marched back to ARRAS. It was an awful march in the dark – the mud was very deep + men had to be dug out of it at times but by 2 A.M. [illegible] into billets.	
			Our casualties during these four days were:–	
			Officers:– Captain C. WHITLEY. M.C. KILLED. LIEUT. F. J. St AUBYN — " — 2nd LIEUT F. R. WILLIAMS — " — " P. F. WALFORD — " — " B. D. FENARD WOUNDED " S. WIGGINS — " —	
			[illegible] G. T. [illegible] M.C. DIED of WOUNDS Lieut K. H. WILLIAMSON — " — LIEUT. C. C. [illegible] Wounded LIEUT. J. G. JOHNSTON, SCOTTISH RIFLES, WOUNDED 2nd Lieut C. E. PULLINGER, WOUNDED — " — W. D. DRING, — " —	
			Other Ranks	

	KILLED	DIED of WOUNDS	WOUNDED	MISSING
Serjeants	1	1	9	1
L/Sgts + Cpls	3	–	6	–
Riflemen	17	14	125	9
Totals	20	15	140	9

This total includes 5 O.R's wounded and to duty.

1577 Wt. W10791/1773 500,000 1/15 D. D. & L. A.D.S.S./Forms/C. 2118.

"A" Form.

Army Form C.2121 (in pads of 100).

MESSAGES AND SIGNALS.

No. of Message........

Prefix ....Code..........m. | Words | Charge | This message is on a/c of: | Recd. at..............m.

Office of Origin and Service Instructions.

Sent At..........m. To.......... By..........

..........Service.

Date.......... From.......... By..........

(Signature of "Franking Officer.")

TO 7/60 ~~8/60th~~ ~~7/RB~~ ~~8 RB.~~ 41st ~~L Bde~~ ~~M G Coy.~~

Sender's Number.	Day of Month.	In reply to Number.	AAA
* B 298.	11/4		

The attack will be renewed tomorrow AAA at 5 am. 3rd Divn advances to attack GUEMAPPE AAA By 6 am 56th Divn hope to be on Hill 90 N 21 d to N.22 C. AAA. at 6 am. 30th & 21st Divns. attack COJEUL SWITCH in N.27, 28 & 34. 30th Divn have further objectives HENINEL and high Ground N.29.b. AAA 41st I Bde will attack WANCOURT at 6.30 am as follows AAA Owing to presence of enemy in BROWN second line it will be necessary to start barrage on BROWN original enemy front line AAA Troop in occupation of BROWN will therefore be withdrawn to the best cover available about 200 to 300 yards in rear by 6.30 am. AAA. Creeping barrage comes down on BROWN original front line

From

Place

Time

The above may be forwarded as now corrected. (Z)

Censor. Signature of Addressor or person authorised to telegraph in his name.

* This line should be erased if not required.

750,000. W 2186—M509. H. W. & V., Ld. 6/16.

"A" Form.

Army Form C.2121
(In pads of 100).

MESSAGES AND SIGNALS.

No. of Message.........

Prefix .... Code .... m.	Words	Charge	This message is on a/c of:	Recd. at........m.
Office of Origin and Service Instructions.	Sent		........Service.	Date........
	At........m.			From........
	To........			
	By........		(Signature of "Franking Officer.")	By........

TO

Sender's Number.	Day of Month.	In reply to Number.	AAA
*			

at 6.30 am and lifts off it at 6.40 am. by which hour leading wave must have advanced again as close under the barrage as possible AAA barrage lifts back at rate of 100 yards in 4 minutes to the N and S line between ~~[illegible]~~ N 23 and N 24 where it remains for 10 minutes and then ceases AAA Northern limit of barage N.16 central to N.18 C.0.0 Southern limit from N.22.a. central to N 24.C.0.5 AAA NO troops of BLUE to be South of line N.23.C.0.6 and N 24.C.0.6 as this ground is likely to be shelled during attack on HENINEL AAA After Capture of WANCOURT 41st I Bde will establish line on high ground N.24.d facing S.E and establish posts connecting with 3rd Divn in O 13.C

From

Place

Time

The above may be forwarded as now corrected. (Z)

Censor. Signature of Addressor or person authorised to telegraph in his name.

* This line should be erased if not required.

750,000. W 2186-1660. H. W. & V., Ld. 6/16.

"A" Form.
Army Form C.2121
(In pads of 100).

MESSAGES AND SIGNALS.

No. of Message

Prefix .... Code .... m. | Words | Charge | This message is on a/c of: .... Service. (Signature of "Franking Officer.") | Recd. at .... m. Date .... From .... By ....

Office of Origin and Service Instructions.

Sent At .... m. To .... By ....

TO

Sender's Number. | Day of Month. | In reply to Number. | AAA

*

~~AAA~~ and with 56th Divn in N.13.a AAA The attack of the 41st I Bde will be carried out as follows AAA In first line 7.KRRC on right 7 RB on left dividing line between battalions road through village from N.23 a 0.6 to Cross Roads in N.23 c.2.4 to 7.KRRC inclusive AAA 8.RB. will cooperate in support AAA 8 KRRC will be in reserve AAA Bde H.Q will remain as at present AAA O.C: M.G Coy will endeavour to keep down enemy fire from HILL 90 N.21 d to N.22.c and high ground to the EAST of WANCOURT until occupied by our troops AAA Should the attack be successful the Division will be prepared to advance.

From
Place BLUE
Time

The above may be forwarded as now corrected. | (Z) G.M. Sinclair Capt.

Censor. | Signature of Addressor or person authorised to telegraph in his name.

* This line should be erased if not required.

750,000. W 2186—M509. H. W. & V., Ld. 6/16.

7th (S) Bn K.R.R.C.

[illegible]

C W Bury

Secret

XVI

41st Inf. Bde.

Herewith Original copy of the War Diary for the month of April 1917.

C W Bury Lt. Col

30/4/1917.

Comdg. 7th K. R. Rifles

"A" Form.

Army Form C.2121 (In pads of 100)

MESSAGES AND SIGNALS.

No. of Message ......

Prefix ...... Code ...... m. | Words | Charge

Office of Origin and Service Instructions

Sent

At ...... m.

To ......

By ......

This message is on a/c of:

...... *Service.*

(Signature of "Franking Officer.")

Recd. at ...... m.

Date ......

From ......

By ......

TO

Sender's Number.	Day of Month.	In reply to Number.	AAA
*			

From

Place

Time

The above may be forwarded as now corrected. (Z)

Censor. Signature of Addressor or person authorised to telegraph in his name.

* This line should be erased if not required.

760,000 W 2186—M509. H. W. & V., Ld. 6/16.

"A" Form.

Army Form C.2121
(In pads of 100).

MESSAGES AND SIGNALS.

No. of Message

Prefix ... Code ... m. Office of Origin and Service Instructions.	Words	Charge	This message is on a/c of: ... Service. (Signature of "Franking Officer.")	Recd. at ... m. Date ... From ... By ...
	Sent At ... m. To ... By ...			

TO 7/6th

Sender's Number.	Day of Month.	In reply to Number.	AAA
* B 386	Ref Map 51 B SW 1/20000		

The objective of the 41st I. Bde is the high ground SE of WANCOURT about N 24 D and O 19. C facing East and North East with posts pushed thence to the COJEUL RIVER to connect with the RIGHT of VI Corps AAA It is understood that the 43rd I Bde have taken the BROWN LINE and are now in occupation of WANCOURT AAA 41st I Bde will in any case relieve the 43rd I Bde ~~of~~ whatever line they are holding and proceed to its own objective AAA 7 KRRC and 7 RB will advance on WANCOURT towards their objective. 7 KRRC to South of village 7 RB to north of it the main village road from N. 23. B 2.4 to N 22 B 90 55 is allotted to 7 RB inclusive. passage through the actual village is to be undertaken

From

Place

Time

The above may be forwarded as now corrected.

(Z)

Censor. Signature of Addressor or person authorised to telegraph in his name.

* This line should be erased if not required.

750,000. W 2186—M509. H. W. & V., Ld. 6/16.

SECRET. D.A.56/10

7th Bn., K.R.R.C.
8th Bn., K.R.R.C.
7th Bn., Rifle Bde.
8th Bn., Rifle Bde.
41st M.G.Coy.

Herewith 1 copy of map showing routes to be taken by tanks.

Please acknowledge.

7/4/17.

D. J. Foxwell Lieut
for Captain,
Brigade Major,
41st Infantry Brigade.

CA 263

Tank routes

S E C R E T.   Copy No....

41st INFANTRY BRIGADE OPERATION ORDER No. 131.

7th April, 1917.

1. In continuation of 41st Infantry Brigade O.O.130 of 5th April, the following additional orders are issued.

2. (i) Maps illustrating the time table for the lifts of the creeping barrages are issued herewith.

(a) Up to and including the capture of the BLUE Line.

(b) From the BLUE LINE to the BROWN LINE.

(ii) The dotted lines indicate the approximate lines on which the barrage will be placed and the figures on or at the end of these lines indicate the time counting from zero hour at which the creeping barrage will lift off the line concerned, i.e. 2.20 indicates 2 hours 20min. after zero.

(iii) The hour + 2 hours 4 min. will be marked by all guns forming the barrage opening with a salvo of shrapnel on the line marked + 2.12.

3. At zero the 3rd Division on our left is advancing to the attack of the German front line system of trenches on their front.

4. At + 3 hours 12min. the creeping barrage lifts off the last portion of the BLUE LINE and goes back to form a protective barrage about 300 yards EAST of the BLUE LINE.

The rate of fire of the protective barrage gradually decreases until + 6 hours 48min. when the advance from the BLUE to the BROWN LINE commences, and at which hour the rate of fire again rises to the rate fixed for the creeping barrage.

5. It is most important for all ranks to realise that to ensure success it is necessary to keep as close to the creeping barrage as possible ready to deal with the defenders of any trench as soon as the barrage lifts off that trench.

6. At 2 hours 4min. after zero the 41st Infantry Brigade will begin its movement from the caves to positions of assembly.

With reference to para 10 of Brigade O.O.No.130 of 5th [illegible] each unit will emerge simultaneously from two only out of the four exits allotted to it.

7. (i) 16 Tanks will assist the attack of the 3rd and 14th Divisions on the Harp, four of which will subsequently assist in the attack on the COJEUL SWITCH.

(ii) All ranks are to be warned that they are on no account to wait for Tanks should the latter get delayed. The advance of the Infantry is to be regulated by the pace of the creeping barrage.

8. (i) As soon as the BLUE LINE is captured one Field Artillery Group will be moved forward to positions about N 12 c to assist in the advance from the BLUE to the BROWN LINE.

(ii) A second Field Artillery Group may be moved up soon after the one mentioned in (i).

9. The R.E. and 2 Companies, Pioneers, will commence work as under as soon after zero + 2 hours as the situation permits.

(a) Construct a tramline on the old German formation level running through M 12, M 18, N 13 and N 14.

(b) Assist the Artillery in construction of gun positions about M 12 c.

(c) Clear the road from BEAURAINS to TELEGRAPH HILL via the cross roads in M 6 c and make two mule tracks, one from HAZEBROUCK STREET to the North of TELEGRAPH HILL, the other from about M 4 d 7.5 past the South of TELEGRAPH HILL to the COJEUL SWITCH.

10. (i) Contact aeroplanes will be in the air from zero to dusk. Distinguishing marks have been issued separately.

(ii) Contact aeroplanes will call by KLAXON HORNS for flares to be lit by the leading troops as nearly as possible at the following hours:-

zero + 3 hours 30min.
" + 7 " 30 "
" + 8 " 30 "
" +11 "

(iii) Only red flares will be used.

11. Medical arrangements have been issued separately.

12. Watches will be synchronised daily by SIGNALS at 9 a.m. and 6 p.m., and on Z day each unit will send a representative with 2 watches to Brigade H.Q. for this purpose at zero.

Issued at 3 p.m.
Copies to:
1. 7th K.R.R.C. *
2. 8th K.R.R.C.
3. 7th R.B.
4. 8th R.B.
5. 41st M.G.Coy.
6. 41st T.M.Bty.
7. 14th Div. G.
8. O.C., Caves.
9. B.T.O.
10. B.S.O.
11. B.I.O.
12. S.C.
13. O.O.File.
14. W.D.

G.M. Lee
Captain,
Brigade Major,
41st Infantry Brigade.

Starred copies only have maps attached

Secret.

War Diary

of

7th (Service) Bn King's Royal Rifle Corps.

from 26th April 1917

to 31st May 1917

(Volume 25)

Instructions regarding War Diaries and Intelligence Summaries are contained in F. S. Regs., Par. II. and the Staff Manual respectively. Title pages will be prepared in manuscript.

WAR DIARY for MAY 1917

~~or~~

~~INTELLIGENCE SUMMARY.~~

(Erase heading not required.)

Army Form C. 2118.

Vol 25

Place	Date	Hour	Summary of Events and Information	Remarks and references to Appendices
In Support	26 Apl to 28 Apl		The Bn moved from Mercatel to Cojeul Switch in Support and remained there until 28th April. The Accommodation & Shelter for the men was very poor but luckily the weather was fine and no undue discomfort was suffered by the Troops. During above time the Bn was employed in cleaning up the area and repairing road from Divn Hqrs in the direction of Wancourt.	AWMG
In the Line	28 Apl to 1 May		Bn moved up to front line & took over from 9th R.B. The disposition of the Battalion was as follows:- 2 Coys in HERON TRENCH 1 Coy in GANNET TRENCH 1 Coy and Bn Hqrs in DUCK TRENCH. The Bn remained in Line until night of 1/2 May and were occupied in improving Trenches providing Covering Parties and digging Assembly Trenches. There was much shelling during this period. Casualties were light.	AWMG
In Support	1 May		On night of 1st/2nd May the Bn was relieved in Line by 8th R.B. and 8th KRRC and moved to NEPAL TRENCH where they remained until night of 3rd May.	AWMG
	2 May		MAJOR J G BIRCH, LT A H HERBERTSON, 2 LT M. W. PETERS, 2 LTs A.J. HOOPER and R.G. LEE joined the Bn. A Draft of 9 OR. from Divisnl Depot Bn also joined the Bn.	AWMG
In Support	3 May	12:30 AM	2 Coys & Bn Hqrs moved up from NEPAL TRENCH to ALBATROSS TRENCH prior to the attack by 8 RB & 8 KRRC. During this Relief the Troops were subjected to Shelling by Tear Shells particularly in the Wancourt Valley	AWMG

A6945 Wt. W11422/M1160 350,000 12/16 D. D. & L. Forms/C.2118/14.

Instructions regarding War Diaries and Intelligence Summaries are contained in F. S. Regs., Par. II. and the Staff Manual respectively. Title pages will be prepared in manuscript.

WAR DIARY
or
INTELLIGENCE SUMMARY.
(Erase heading not required.)

Army Form C. 2118.

Place	Date	Hour	Summary of Events and Information	Remarks and references to Appendices
	3 May	3.45 AM	Our Barrage commenced sharp to time. It was an exceptionally dark morning & from Albatross Trench the flashes of the Guns presented a wonderful sight, one saw nothing but a mazes of flashes stretching as far as the eyes could see. About Zero + 30 orders were received to send 1 Coy to Curlew Trench, 1 Coy to Buzzard Trench & for the remaining 2 Coys in Hepal Trench to move up to Albatross Trench, these [illegible] were immediately made. During the whole of the day the [illegible] very heavy Artillery fire especially round Albatross Trench [illegible] Valley. There was a few Casualties including 1 Officer [illegible] At about 8.30 pm Orders were received to relieve the 8th RB and [illegible] in the Line. this Relief was successfully carried out.	
	4 May	3.30 AM	Bn HQrs in Heron Trench was shelled causing 6 Casualties & considerable confusion. The remainder of the day was fairly quiet	
	5 May		On the night of 5/6 May the Bn was relieved by 6 KOYLI, during this Relief the Bn was subjected to very heavy Shell fire which commenced about 10 PM & lasted until dawn, It is a remarkable fact that although the Relief took place over the open only 2 Casualties were suffered.	

A6945 Wt. W11422/M1160 350,000 12/16 D. D. & L. Forms/C. 2118/14.

Instructions regarding War Diaries and Intelligence Summaries are contained in F. S. Regs., Part II. and the Staff Manual respectively. Title Pages will be prepared in manuscript.

WAR DIARY ~~or INTELLIGENCE SUMMARY~~ for May 1917.

(Erase heading not required.)

Army Form C. 2118.

Vol 25

Place	Date	Hour	Summary of Events and Information	Remarks and references to Appendices
	5		On Relief the Bn moved to trenches about N15C and was immediately placed at the disposal of 43 I.B	AMG
	6		Draft of 22 O.R. joined from Divisional Depot Bn.	
			from 6 May to 14th the Bn was employed in Digging trenches the casualties during this period were rather heavy.	AMG
	11		2 Lt J.P. ELLSMOOR rejoined Bn from Field Ambulance	AMG
	12		Lt F.W. EMERSON " " " 41st T.M.B	
			2 Lt W.O. DRING " " " Wounds. Draft of 11 O.R. joined from Divisional Depot Bn.	AMG
	13		2 Lt F.H. NEWMAN joined Bn 2 Lt G.B. MOUNTFORD admitted to Field Ambulance.	AMG
In the Line	14		Lt H.A. HORSBURGH, general List, joined Bn	
			The Bn relieved the 6 KOYLI in front line, 3 Coys in front Line and 1 Coy in Support	AMG
	15		2 Lt E.G. BUTTFIELD joined Bn.	AMG
	16		CAPT. E FAIRLIE rejoined Bn from 9th KRRC. LT A.H. HERBERTSON, 1 Cpl & 1 OR went out on Patrol and failed to return	AMG
	17		On the night of 16/17 one of our advanced Patrols observed 4 Enemy approaching carrying 2 Machine Guns, when the enemy Patrol had advanced near enough our Patrol attacked them killing 1 of the enemy and wounded 2 whom they took Prisoners together with 2 Machine Guns and 1 Tripod. Much useful information	AMG

2449 Wt. W14957/M90 750,000 1/16 J.B.C. & A. Forms/C.2118/12.

Instructions regarding War Diaries and Intelligence Summaries are contained in F. S. Regs., Part II, and the Staff Manual respectively. Title pages will be prepared in manuscript.

WAR DIARY
or
INTELLIGENCE SUMMARY.
(Erase heading not required.)

Army Form C. 2118.

Vol 23

Place	Date	Hour	Summary of Events and Information	Remarks and references to Appendices
	17		was obtained. On night of 17/18 a Bombing Patrol consisting of 1 NCO & 7 [illegible] went out to Bomb a German Sap. The O/C of Party failed to return but eventually turned up on the night of 19th inst after an adventurous career. After having thrown a Bomb at his objective he turned to come in and took the wrong direction along the road & got into a trench which he thought was ours, on hearing foreign tongues he got out and as day was breaking he dug himself in behind the trench in a Shell Hole. He reported that our firing on the German trench ([illegible] Trench) and our Stokes & Rifle Grenades on the German Sap were very effective.	
	18		On the night of 15th a Prisoner was captured belonging to 4th Coy 84th R.I.R. During this tour the situation was fairly quiet with the exception of the left Coy in front line & Bn HQrs which received a fair amount of ~~[illegible]~~ Shell [illegible]	
	19		On the night of 19th the Bn was relieved by 8 K.R.R.C. and went into support 1 Coy in EGRET TRENCH 1 in DUCK 1 Coy & Bn HQrs in the NEST and 1 Coy in NEPAL TRENCH, where they remained until night of 24/25th. During this time the Bn was employed in carrying trench Mortar Bombs, Trench Boards and digging a new support trench.	

A6945 Wt. W11422/M1160 350,000 12/16 D. D. & L. Forms/C.2118/14.

Instructions regarding War Diaries and Intelligence Summaries are contained in F. S. Regs., Part II, and the Staff Manual respectively. Title pages will be prepared in manuscript.

WAR DIARY for May 1917.

~~or~~ ~~INTELLIGENCE SUMMARY.~~

(Erase heading not required.)

Army Form C. 2118.

Vol 25.

Place	Date	Hour	Summary of Events and Information	Remarks and references to Appendices
	21		CAPT E.C. BLAND admitted to F.A.	[initials]
	22		LT COL G.A.P. RENNIE D.S.O. rejoined the Bn	[initials]
	23		LT J F BEWEN, LT P.L. DAVIES and 2LT D M HUTTON joined Bn.	[initials]
	24		On night of 24/25 the Bn moved into NEPAL TRENCH	[initials]
Beaurains	25		The Bn moved to Beaurains in Divisional Reserve.	[initials]
"	26		Lt Col C.K. HOWARD-BURY proceeded to take over command of 9 K.R.R.C	[initials]
"	27		Training	[initials]
"	28		Draft of 70 O.R. joined Bn from Divisional Depot Bn.	[initials]
"	29		Training	[initials]
"	30		Training	[initials]
"	31		~~Training~~ Our Casualties during May were as follows.	

	Officers				Other Ranks			
	KILLED	DIED OF WOUNDS	WOUNDED	MISSING	KILLED	DIED OF WOUNDS	WOUNDED	MISSING
2Lt G.A. CARR	–	–	1	–	16	2	63*	2
LT A.H. HERBERTSON	–	–	–	1				

* 3 of whom were wounded + to duty.

G. Rennie, Lt Col.
Comdg 7th Bn K.R. Rifles

A6945 Wt. W11422/M1160 350,000 12/16 D. D. & L. Forms/C./2118/14.

7th (Service) Bn King's Royal Rifles.

The average strength of Battalion during month of May was

33 Officers 935 Other Ranks

2 Officers & 41 Other Ranks were admitted to F. A during the month of whom 14 other ranks evacuated the Divisional Area, & 6 other ranks rejoined the Battn.

31/5/17.

G. Rennie. Lt Col
Comdg 7 (S) Bn
King's Royal Rifles

Secret

Vol 25.

7th (Service) Battalion

The King's Royal Rifle Corps

War Diary

from 26 - 5 - 1917.

to 30 - 6 - 1917.

Volume 26.

Secret

41st Inf. Bde.

Herewith the original copy of the War Diary of the Battalion under my command for the period 26/5/19 to 30/6/19

G. Rennie. Lt Col

Comdg 7th K R Rifles

30/6/19

(6414) Wt. W3990/P1807 2,500,000 7/18 McA & W Ltd (E 3591) Forms W3091/4. Army Form W.3091.

196

Cover for Documents.

VOL. 28

Nature of Enclosures.

7th Bn K.R.R.C.

1-6-17

to

30-6-17

7th Bn Kings Royal Rifle C.

198

The average strength of the Bn during the month of June 1917 was 36 Officers 924 Other Ranks

1 Officer & 25 Other Ranks were admitted to hospital during the month of June. 8 O.R. [illegible] [illegible] 21 [illegible] Bn

R. [illegible]

Instructions regarding War Diaries and Intelligence Summaries are contained in F. S. Regs., Part II. and the Staff Manual respectively. Title Pages will be prepared in manuscript.

WAR DIARY

(Erase heading not required.)

VOL. 26.

Army Form C. 2118.

JUNE 1917 to Dec 1917

Place	Date	Hour	Summary of Events and Information	Remarks and references to Appendices
BEAURAINS	26.6.17		2nd Lt G.B. MOUNTFORD M.C. invalided to England.	Ra[illegible]
"	June 30th		Battalion in Divisional Reserve at BEAURAINS.	Ra[illegible]
NEPAL TRENCH	1st		Battalion relieved 9th K.R.R. in NEPAL TRENCH [illegible]	[illegible]
"	3rd		CAPTAIN E.C. BLAND invalided to England. Battalion found working parties [illegible]	[illegible]
"	6th		[illegible] O.R. joined Battalion from Divisional Depot Battalion.	[illegible]
"	9th		Battalion relieved in NEPAL TRENCH by 6th K.O.Y.L.I. & marched to BEAURAINS	[illegible]
BEAURAINS	10th		Battalion in Brigade Reserve.	[illegible]
"	11th		Battalion marched to MONCHIET in the early morning [illegible] whole of the march, but cleared up [illegible] the battalion [illegible] billeted in huts.	[illegible]
MONCHIET	12th		Battalion marched to SAULTY in the morning [illegible] accommodated in billets.	[illegible]
SAULTY	13th		Battalion marched to LOUVENCOURT in the early morning. The weather [illegible] march was pleasant. The Battalion is accommodated in [illegible] billets.	[illegible]
LOUVENCOURT	14th		Battalion in rest in LOUVENCOURT. Training [illegible].	[illegible]
"	26th		Divisional Horse Show at MARIEUX. A [illegible] The first prize for officers chargers was won by Colonel R[illegible].	[illegible]
"	27th		Brigade Sports were held at BERTRANCOURT in the afternoon. The Battalion [illegible] the Boxing Competition, [illegible] Competitions [illegible]	[illegible]
"	29th		Training [illegible]	[illegible]
"	30th		Brigade [illegible] the entire day. Brigade Field Day.	[illegible]

G. R[illegible] Lt Col.
Commanding [illegible]

2449 Wt. W14957/M90 750,000 1/16 J.B.C. & A. Forms/C.2118/12.

Instructions regarding War Diaries and Intelligence Summaries are contained in F. S. Regs., Part II. and the Staff Manual respectively. Title Pages will be prepared in manuscript.

WAR DIARY
or
~~INTELLIGENCE SUMMARY~~
(Erase heading not required.)

VOL. 26. Army Form C. 2118.

JUNE 1917.

Place	Date	Hour	Summary of Events and Information	Remarks and references to Appendices
BEAURAINS	26.5.17		2nd Lt G.B. MOUNTFORD MC invalided to England.	Paul.
"	June 1st		Battalion in Divisional Reserve at BEAURAINS.	Paul.
NEPAL TRENCH	" 2nd		Battalion relieved 9th K.R.R. in NEPAL TRENCH & came under the orders of the 42nd I.B.	Paul.
"	" 3rd		CAPTAIN E.C. BLAND invalided to England. Battalion finds working parties for 42nd I.B.	Paul.
"	" 6th		17 O.R. joined Battalion from Divisional Depot Battalion.	Paul.
"	" 9th		Battalion relieved in NEPAL TRENCH by 6th K.S.L.I. & marched to BEAURAINS	Paul.
BEAURAINS	" 10th		Battalion in Brigade Reserve	Paul.
"	" 11th		Battalion marched to MONCHIET, in the early morning. It poured with rain during the whole of the march, but cleared up as soon as the battalion got in. We were billeted in huts.	Paul.
MONCHIET.	" 12th		Battalion marched to SAULTY in the morning & was accommodated in billets.	Paul.
SAULTY.	" 13th		Battalion marched to LOUVENCOURT in the early morning. The weather was fine & march was pleasant. The Battalion is accommodated in good billets.	Paul.
LOUVENCOURT	14th		Battalion in rest in LOUVENCOURT. Training proceeding.	Paul.
"	26th		Divisional Horse Show at MARIEUX. A great success. The whole battalion was present. The first prize for Officers chargers was won by Colonel Rennie.	Paul.
"	27th		Brigade Sports were held at BERTRANCOURT in the afternoon. The Battalion won the Bombing Competition, Field Marching Order Race & was second in the Stretcher bearers Competition & third in the Lewis gun, Signallers & Buglers Competition.	Paul.
"	29th		Training in all its various forms continues. Brigade Sports the entire day.	
"	30		Brigade Field Day	Paul. WMG

G. Rennie. Lt Col.
Comdg 7th Bn K R Rifles

2449 Wt. W14957/M90 750,000 1/16 J.B.C. & A. Forms/C.2118/12.

4th (S) Kings Royal Rifle Batt.

The ration strength of the Bn during the month of June 1917 was 36 Officers 927 Other Ranks.

1 Officer & 39 O. Ranks were admitted to hospital during the month of June. 8 Other Ranks evacuated by 21 [illegible] Amb.

30/6/17.

A. Rennie. Lt-Col
Comdg 4th (S) Bn
K. R. Rifles.

Secret.

7th (Service) Battalion,

The King's Royal Rifle Corps.

War Diary

From 1st to 31st July 1917.

Volume 27

Instructions regarding War Diaries and Intelligence Summaries are contained in F. S. Regs., Part II. and the Staff Manual respectively. Title pages will be prepared in manuscript.

WAR DIARY for JULY 1917

~~or~~

~~INTELLIGENCE SUMMARY.~~

(Erase heading not required.)

Army Form C. 2118.

Volume 27.

Place	Date	Hour	Summary of Events and Information	Remarks and references to Appendices
FRANCE				
In the Field	July 1st 1917		Bn in billets at LOUVENCOURT.	
			MAJOR RAMSAY to Senior Officers Course ALDERSHOT. MAJOR T.G. BIRCH assumed the duties of 2nd in Command.	
	6th		2nd Lt G.H. BARNES joined on posting	
	10th	7.20am	Bn. marched to Billets at BEAUVAL	
	11th	9.30pm	Bn. marched to Stn. at DOULLENS & entrained at 12 [illegible] am for GODEWAERSVELDE	
	12th		Bn marched to CLARE CAMP near LOCRE arriving at [illegible] am	
	15th		Lt E.V. SAPP and 2/Lt T.R. BRETT [illegible] to Bn. on [illegible] [illegible] England [illegible]	
	[illegible]		2/Lt S. PYE joined the Bn. on posting [illegible] ORs wounded [illegible]	
	23rd		Lt J.F.B. SWAN to R.F.C. on probation as observer. 2/Lt [illegible] [illegible] VINCENT and J.W. SHAW, MC joined the Bn on posting.	
	24th		2/Lt C.E. PULLINGER, MC rejoined the Bn from [illegible]	
	25th		Lt E.V. SAPP left for England for [illegible] re commission in Indian Army	
	29th		Capt ASHWORTH returned from course at [illegible] Army School [illegible]	
	30th		Bn marched to FRONTIER CAMP	

A6945 Wt. W11422/M1160 350,000 12/16 D. D. & L. Forms/C. 2118/14.

[illegible] Lt.Col.
Comdg [illegible]

7th (S) Bn King's Royal Rifles.

The average strength of the Battn during July 1917 was

Officers 36 Other Ranks 959

1 Officers & 46 Other Ranks were admitted to Field Ambulance during the month of whom.
1 Officer was invalided to England
11 Other Ranks were evacuated from the Divisional Area & 23 Other Ranks rejoined the Battn.

31/7/17

G. Rennie. Lieut Col
Comd'g 7th (S) Bn
King's Royal Rifles

Secret

1st (Service) Battalion

The King's Royal Rifle Corps.

4/14

War Diary

From 1st to 31st August 1917

Volume 28

Instructions regarding War Diaries and Intelligence Summaries are contained in F. S. Regs., Part II. and the Staff Manual respectively. Title pages will be prepared in manuscript.

WAR DIARY for AUGUST 1917
~~or~~
~~INTELLIGENCE SUMMARY.~~
(Erase heading not required.)

Army Form C. 2118.

Volume 28

Place	Date	Hour	Summary of Events and Information	Remarks and references to Appendices
	AUG			
	1st		Bn remains at FRONTIER CAMP.	JMB
	3rd		Lt B.H. SUMNER attached Military Intelligence Directorate, W.O. on probation	JMB
	5th		Capt E.H. HANKS 2/7 London Regt rejoined Bn. for duty from T.M. IVERGNY	JMB.
	7th		2/Lt R.G. LEE, London Regt admitted to F.A.	JMB
HONDEGHEM	6th		Bn. marched into billets near HONDEGHEM. Bn in GHQ. Reserve	JMB
	7th		Lt E.V. SAPP. Medical Board ordered by W.O. Struck off strength of Bn.	JMB.
	6th–15th		Bn. remained in good billets near HONDEGHEM, and carried out coy. training in grass fields. A certain amount of football & cricket was played, and the inhabitants were unusually accomodating	MJSA.
DICKEBUSCH	15th		Bn. moved by train from CAESTRE to OUDERDOM and marched to camp at DICKEBUSCH arriving about midnight	MJSA
TRENCHES	16th		Following upon an unsuccessful attack by other divisions on INVERNESS & GLENCORSE woods the Bn. moved into Brigade	MJSA
	17th		reserve at ZILLEBEKE BUND and on the following day took over our trenches N of MENIN road in J13 and J14 sheet 28. Dispositions – 2½ coys. in front line and immediate support, Bn. HQ and 1½ coys in part of a tunnel built under the MENIN road by the Germans from HOOGE to INVERNESS copse. 7th R.B on our right, 42nd T.B. on our left. Divisions relieved 18th and 56th.	
			The line was in a very bad state after the recent heavy fighting, the approaches were very difficult and the whole area very much shelled. There was no infantry action during this tour, and attention was concentrated on improving	

A6945 Wt. W11422/M1160 350,000 12/16 D. D. & L. Forms/C./2118/14.

Instructions regarding War Diaries and Intelligence Summaries are contained in F. S. Regs., Part II. and the Staff Manual respectively. Title Pages will be prepared in manuscript.

WAR DIARY
or
~~INTELLIGENCE SUMMARY~~

(Erase heading not required.)

for August 1917

Army Form C. 2118.

Volume 28

Place	Date	Hour	Summary of Events and Information	Remarks and references to Appendices
			trenches. Casualties 3 O.R. killed 23 O.R. wounded.	
DICKEBUSCH	20th		Bn. was relieved by 69 B.C.L.I. and moved to Camp at DICKEBUSCH expecting to remain there about 8 days. Owing however to the course of the operations we had a series of moves at very short notice, moving on the 22nd to CHATEAU	WJM
CHATEAU SEGARD	22nd		SEGARD, back again to DICKEBUSCH the next day, and the following morning on a sudden order due to a successful	
DICKEBUSCH	23rd			
Trenches	24th		German counter attack we were sent to the ECOLE YPRES in motor lorries, and finally after a good deal of uncertainty we took over the same line and came under orders of the 43rd I.B., 7th R.B. on our right, 42nd I.B. on our left relieved the next day by 8th R.B. The whole sector then came under command of the 41st I.B. The situation was much the same as when we left, and we still held the important ridge which the Germans were anxious to get back owing to its great command of the country behind our lines.	WJM
	24th		On the first night we sent out patrols to see if any local advance would be possible, but it was found that the Germans were holding their trenches too strongly; on the following night in conjunction with the Bns. on our flanks we were successful in establishing a line of posts, and following on this strong fighting patrols were sent out against the German front trenches but no advance was possible. Either as a result of this activity or in accordance with a prearranged plan	
	25th			
	26th		the enemy attacked early on the 26th, but were successfully repulsed. B Coy suffered rather heavily, the casualties 2/Lieut A.J. Hooper killed, Captain P.K. Haworth & C.S.M. Smith wounded. The same evening we received	WJM
	27th		orders to make a combined attack with the Bns. on our flanks at dawn the following day. Each Bn. was to put in about 1½ platoons, and the main part of the work was to be done by Tanks. Shortly before the attack a supplementary order was received that the attack was to take place even if the Tanks did not arrive. Rain had fallen heavily for some hours, and the state of the ground was very bad. The Tanks arrived at the rendezvous but were unable to proceed. 2/Lieut C.E. Pillinger who was in command of our party was wounded before the attack started, and owing to the state of the ground and enemy M.G. fire, it was not possible to make an advance.	WJM

2449 Wt. W14957/M90 750,000 1/16 J.B.C. & A. Forms/C.2118/12.

Instructions regarding War Diaries and Intelligence Summaries are contained in F. S. Regs., Part II. and the Staff Manual respectively. Title Pages will be prepared in manuscript.

WAR DIARY
or
INTELLIGENCE SUMMARY
(Erase heading not required.)

Army Form C. 2118.

August 1917

Vol 28

Place	Date	Hour	Summary of Events and Information	Remarks and references to Appendices
Trenches	27th		About 6 pm we heard that we were to be relieved and the advance officers of 33rd Div. had just arrived when about 8 pm the enemy put down a very heavy barrage followed by a general attack on the ridge. This was repulsed and we took 2 prisoners.	
DICKEBUSCH			Afterwards the relief proceeded quietly and Bn. moved to DICKEBUSCH camp, and the following day to billets near	MJSA.
METEREN	28th		METEREN where the remainder of the month was spent in cleaning and reorganising.	
			Casualties 24th – 27th Killed 2/Lieut A. J. HOOPER and 16 O.R.	
			Wounded. Capt. P. K. HAWORTH, 2/Lieut C. E. PULLINGER M.C., 2/Lieut H. G. BARNES and 71 O.R.	
			Missing. 6 O.R.	MJSA.
	11th		Capt. E. H. HANKS 2/19th London Regt (attached to Bn.) appointed to temp. command of 2nd Army garrison Coy.	
	15th		Lt B. H. Sumner struck off strength Employed at Military Intelligence Directorate War Office.	MJSA.
	18th		Capt. E. Page M.C. attached 14th Div. for instruction was appointed Staff Captain 17th I.B. [illegible] 1917	
	13th		Lt C. H. D. King to F.A.	
	19th		Lt. J. N. Martin joined Div. Depot Bn. from wounds.	MJSA.
	20th		2/Lieut F. C. Vincent to F.A. rejoined 26th	
	27th		2/Lieuts A/St. J. Rose & S. Pye to F.A.	MJSA.
	28th		2/Lieut F. L. Trotter joined Bn.	

G. Rennie Lieut Col
Cmdg 7th K.R. Rifles
1.9.17.

2449 Wt. W14957/M90 750,000 1/16 J.B.C. & A. Forms/C.2118/12.

4th Bn. King's Royal Rifles

The average strength of Battalion during the month of August was 32 Officers & 884 Other Ranks. Of whom 5 Officers & 45 O.R's were admitted to Field Ambulances, 3 Officers & 25 Other Ranks were evacuated out of the Divisional Area, 1 Officer & 5 O.R's rejoined from Field Ambulance & 1 Officer & 15 O.R's still remain in Field Ambulance.

1/9/17

G. Reade
Lieut-Col
Comdg 4th Battalion
King's Royal Rifles

Secret

War Diary

of

7th (Service) Battalion

The King's Royal Rifle Corps

From 1st Sep. to 30th Sep. 1917

Volume 29

Instructions regarding War Diaries and Intelligence Summaries are contained in F. S. Regs., Part II. and the Staff Manual respectively. Title pages will be prepared in manuscript.

WAR DIARY or ~~INTELLIGENCE~~ SUMMARY.

(Erase heading not required.)

SEPTEMBER

Army Form C. 2118.

Place	Date	Hour	Summary of Events and Information	Remarks and references to Appendices
METEREN	1st		Bn. at rest. From there we moved on the 2nd into the VIII Corps area, first to WATERLOO CAMP	M.J.M.
WATERLOO CAMP	2nd		and then on to NEUVE EGLISE which it was understood was to be our permanent rest billet for	M.J.M.
NEUVE EGLISE	5th		the winter. The Division took over the line E. of MESSINES and started with one Brigade at a time in the line	
			Lieut J. N. Martin rejoined on the 1st, but left to command the Div. Convalescent Coy on the 7th. 2/Lieut W. A. Knight joined on the 6th but went to hospital on the 20th. 8 O.R. joined on 5th and 1 O.R. was killed (self inflicted) on the 7th.	M.J.M.
MESSINES	12th		The Bn moved into Bde support. Bn. & Coy HQ were accommodated in Pill Boxes. Bn. was finding nightly working parties. Movement in daylight had to be restricted on the Messines ridge, but a very fine view was obtained of towns in rear of the German lines. The line was fairly quiet though the proximity of some of our own batteries caused some annoyance, and was always likely to draw retaliation. Casualties for the 4 days. 3 O.R. killed 5 O.R. wounded, nearly all by one salvo on a party was returning from work.	M.J.M.
Front Line	16th		Bn relieved 8th R.B. holding front line from the BLAUWEPOORTBEEK 28 O 29 c 5 0 to 28 U 5 B central. The line was in bad condition, it was difficult to get round in daylight, and very little existed in the way of adequate support or reserve lines. B, C, D Coys in front line and A in support. 7th R.B. on	

A6945 Wt. W11422/M1160 350,000 12/16 D. D. & L. Forms/C.2118/14.

Instructions regarding War Diaries and Intelligence Summaries are contained in F. S. Regs., Par. II. and the Staff Manual respectively. Title pages will be prepared in manuscript.

WAR DIARY
or
INTELLIGENCE SUMMARY.
(Erase heading not required.)

Army Form C. 2118.

Place	Date	Hour	Summary of Events and Information	Remarks and references to Appendices
			the right, 30th Div on left. During this time our artillery fire was very considerable in connection with operations	
			to the North. The 7th R.B. also carried out a successful raid in which B Coy cooperated by exposing	
			dummy figures which gained their object by drawing a good deal of fire.	
			Casualties for the 4 days. 2/Lieut W.O. Doig wounded 19 O.R. wounded.	MJSA.
NEUVE EGLISE	20th		Bn. was relieved by 10th D.L.I. and moved to Neuve Eglise where the remainder of the month was spent in	
			training, and in finding working parties.	MJSA.
	14th		Lieut D. Allhusen joined.	MJSA.
	15th		Lieut C.H.D. King M.C. marked P.B.	MJSA.
	17th		2/Lieut R.G. Lee 8th London Regt. attached invalided to England.	MJSA.
	25th		2/Lieut D.O. Paget & 8 O.R joined.	MJSA.
	28th		2/Lieut R.I. Cowan joined.	MJSA.
	29th		14 O.R. joined.	MJSA.

J.P. Birch Major
Cmdg 7th K.R.Rifles.

A6945 Wt. W11422/M1160 350,000 12/16 D. D. & L. Forms/C./2118/14.

7th (S.) Bn. King's Royal Rifle Corps

The average strength of Battalion during the month of September 1917 was 30 Officers - 856 Other Ranks.

Of above 1 Officer and 74 Other Ranks were admitted to Field Ambulance, 1 Officer and 12 Other Ranks were evacuated out of the Divisional Area, 38 Other Ranks rejoined from Field Ambulance, and 24 Other Ranks still remain in Field Ambulance.

30th September 1917.

J. Birch
Major
Comdg 7th (S) Battalion
King's Royal Rifle Corps

CONFIDENTIAL.

WAR DIARY

- of -

7th (S) Bn., KING'S ROYAL RIFLE CORPS.

From: 1st October, 1917.
To: 31st October, 1917.

Volume XXX.

Vol 29

Instructions regarding War Diaries and Intelligence Summaries are contained in F. S. Regs., Par. II. and the Staff Manual respectively. Title pages will be prepared in manuscript.

WAR DIARY
or
INTELLIGENCE SUMMARY.
(Erase heading not required.)

Army Form C. 2118.

Place	Date	Hour	Summary of Events and Information	Remarks and references to Appendices
NEUVE EGLISE	1st		Bn in Div Reserve. It was expected that Neuve Eglise would be our winter Headquarters, and much work was done on improvement of billets, roofing a concert hall, and making [illegible] standings. We were expecting to [illegible] into the [illegible] sector on the 6th, but on the previous day all orders were cancelled and we moved in the	
RENINGHELST	6th		afternoon of the 6th to huts near Reninghelst. The weather was very bad and we were living in [illegible] accomodation. 3 days later we moved to camp near DICKEBUSCH and the following day [illegible] to take over	
DICKEBUSCH	9th			
Trenches	10th		the front line from the 1st Bedfords, 5th Division.	
			The relief was carried out under considerable difficulties owing to heavy shell fire and [illegible] of the guides. Two of our company commanders with their headquarters and a whole platoon had to spend a most uncomfortable night in Dumbarton Lakes.	
			Dispositions. Bn held front from MENIN ROAD 28 J 21 D to the SCHERRIAB BEEK. 4th Middlesex on our right, 7th R.B. on our left. Two companies in front line and two in support. [illegible] 14th [illegible] 24th [illegible] [illegible] on our right.	
			The tour of 6 days was most unpleasant, communications were very difficult especially to the [illegible] and [illegible] Road which with the principal routes was always liable to be heavily shelled. The [illegible] [illegible] [illegible] R.S.M. [illegible] severely wounded and [illegible] C.Q.M.S. – [illegible] Stewart and [illegible] – killed [illegible] [illegible] [illegible] men were among the [illegible] of the battalion and [illegible] was very much felt.	

Instructions regarding War Diaries and Intelligence Summaries are contained in F. S. Regs., Part II. and the Staff Manual respectively. Title pages will be prepared in manuscript.

WAR DIARY
or
INTELLIGENCE SUMMARY.
(Erase heading not required.)

Army Form C. 2118.

Place	Date	Hour	Summary of Events and Information	Remarks and references to Appendices
			A large number of men were sick in the line, largely owing to the bad conditions of the trenches, and the impossibility of getting up thigh boots or hot food. We had nearly 70 cases of men sent to F.A. with Trench feet.	
			There were more opportunities for sniping than we had ever had before, as the Germans walked about freely at dawn and dusk. Our men thoroughly enjoyed themselves and accounted for a large number.	
			Our total casualties for the tour were 27 O.R. killed 59 wounded 4 missing.	MJSA
RIDGE WOOD	16th		The Bn. was relieved by 5th Oxf. and Bucks and moved to Camp at RIDGE WOOD. Two days were spent in reorganizing and cleaning.	
	18th		On the 18th Lieut Col. G.A.P. Rennie D.S.O. who had raised the Bn., and except for 3 months had commanded it throughout left to take command of the 146th Inf Bde. 49th Div.	MJSA
BEDFORD House	19th		Bn moved to BEDFORD HOUSE in tactical support to 42nd I.B. and found carrying parties. We were lucky in having only 3 O.R. wounded.	MJSA
LA CLYTTE	22nd		Bn was relieved by 5th Div and moved to Camp near La Clytte. After staying one night we moved into Corps	MJSA
METEREN	23rd		reserve at PHINCBOOM near METEREN. The accommodation was very bad, most of the men being in tents, & little material being available for improvements. The remainder of the month was spent in training – our numbers were very much reduced, and attention was chiefly directed to training men in special branches.	
			An inter-platoon football competition was started, and we had an excellent concert one night from the 9th Bn. Concert party.	MJSA

A6945 Wt. W11422/M1160 350,000 12/16 D. D. & L. Forms/C./2118/14.

[illegible] Royal Rifles

The average strength of Battn during the month of October 1917 was 30 Officers and [illegible] Other Ranks.

Of above 2 Officers and 121 Other Ranks were admitted to F.A., 12 Other Ranks were evacuated out of the Divisional Area, 15 Other Ranks rejoined from F.A. and 2 Officers and 92 Other Ranks still remain in F.A.

[signature]

31st October 1917

Major
Comdg 1st Battalion
Kings Royal Rifle Corps

Secret

Vol 30

War Diary

of

7th (Service) Bn.

The King's Royal Rifle Corps.

From 1st to 30th
November, 1917

Volume 31

Instructions regarding War Diaries and Intelligence Summaries are contained in F. S. Regs., Part II. and the Staff Manual respectively. Title pages will be prepared in manuscript.

WAR DIARY
or
INTELLIGENCE SUMMARY.
(Erase heading not required.)

Army Form C. 2118.

[illegible]

Place	Date	Hour	Summary of Events and Information	Remarks and references to Appendices
METEREN	1st		Lieut. Col. T. E. BIRCH assumed command of the [illegible]	
			Capt. E. FAIRLIE appointed Second in Command of [illegible]	
			proceeded there to take up duties.	
LONGUENESSE	11th		Bn. moved from METEREN by [illegible] [illegible]	
			& Bn. arrived at WIZERNES and marched to [illegible] [illegible]	
			Accommodation good	
	12th		Training continued. Country around the village [illegible]	
	16th		Training. Tournament by companies [illegible]	
	18th		matches were played	
	19th		Bn. carried out Bn. scheme in morning	
	21st		Brigade scheme	
	22nd		Training continued during mornings. Afternoons [illegible] and	
	25th		[illegible]	
	29th		Brigade Relay Race	
BRANDHOEK	30th		Bn. marched from LONGUENESSE – starting at 5.45 am – to [illegible]	
			there it was entrained for BRANDHOEK, then arrived at BRANDHOEK [illegible]	

A6945 Wt. W11422/M1160 350,000 12/16 D. D. & L. Forms/C. 2118/14.

Instructions regarding War Diaries and Intelligence Summaries are contained in F. S. Regs., Par. II. and the Staff Manual respectively. Title pages will be prepared in manuscript.

WAR DIARY
or
INTELLIGENCE SUMMARY.
(Erase heading not required.)

Army Form C. 2118.

Place	Date	Hour	Summary of Events and Information	Remarks and references to Appendices
			about 11.30 am Bn. marched to VLAMERTINGHE and took up billets	K.F.
			in the village. Accommodation poor owing to ruinous state of village.	
			During the month the following officers:-	
			Joined on Posting:- Lt. R. B. SCHOLFIELD + 2nd Lt. T. W. PEARSON 9/11/17; 2nd Lt.	
			F. EVANS + 2nd Lt. S. CLARCE 16/11/17; 2nd Lt. C. R. MOORE 22/11/17.	K.F.
			Invalided to England:- 2nd Lt. J. R. Brett 29/10/17. (sick); 2nd Lieut. S. PYE	
			10/11/17 (Sick)	K.F.
			Rejoined from Hospital:- 2nd Lt. N. A. KNIGHT.	K.F.
			Admitted to F.A.:- 2nd Lt. A. ALLEN (sick)	
			During this month:-	K.F.
			The following drafts joined from D.D.B:- 4/11/17 4 O.R.; 8/11/17 6 O.R.; 14/11/17 6 O.R.;	
			25/11/17 6 O.R.; 19/11/17 5 O.R. Total 27 O.R.	K.F.
			Self inflicted wounds:- 1 O.R.	K.F.
			J. B. Birch Lt. Col.	

Instructions regarding War Diaries and Intelligence Summaries are contained in F. S. Regs., Part II. and the Staff Manual respectively. Title pages will be prepared in manuscript.

WAR DIARY
or
INTELLIGENCE SUMMARY.
(Erase heading not required.)

Army Form C. 2118.

Place	Date	Hour	Summary of Events and Information	Remarks and references to Appendices
			The following officers were evacuated to England: Capt. P. R. Haworth M.C. [illegible] 2/Lieut. [illegible]	
			Lieut. C.H.D. King M.C. rejoined from the Base, and the following officers joined [illegible] 2/Lieuts. [illegible]	
			C. [illegible], J. [illegible] and J. A. [illegible]	
			[illegible] Major	
			Commdg [illegible]	

A6945 Wt. W11422/M1160 350,000 12/16 D. D. & L. Forms/C.2118/14.

7th (S.) Bn. Kings Royal Rifle Corps

The average strength of Battalion during the month of November 1917 was 40 Officers 679 Other Ranks

During the month:-

Offs	O.R.	
1	32	were admitted to F.A.
-	4	" evacuated out of the Divl. area
-	11	rejoined from F.A.
1	17	of those admitted during November remain in F.A.

30th November 1917. Lieut. Col.

Comdg. 7th (S) Bn. K.R.R.C.

Secret

War Diary

of the

7th (Service) Battn.

The King's Royal Rifle Corps

Volume 32

From 1st to 31st Dec. 1917

VOL. 32

Instructions regarding War Diaries and Intelligence Summaries are contained in F. S. Regs., Par. II. and the Staff Manual respectively. Title pages will be prepared in manuscript.

Original

WAR DIARY for DECEMBER 1917

~~INTELLIGENCE SUMMARY.~~

(Erase heading not required.)

Army Form C. 2118.

Place	Date	Hour	Summary of Events and Information	Remarks and references to Appendices
VLAMERTINGHE	1st		Bn. was in billets at Vlamertinghe and entrained on the 2nd at Brandhoek, detrained at Wieltje and after stopping a few	
CALIFORNIA CAMP	2nd		hours at Junction Camp moved to California Camp. The Bn. remained here four days and found working parties on	
			one of which 2/Lieut P.C. Stearns was killed.	MJSA
Trenches	5th		On the night 5th/6th we relieved the 8th Bn. in front of PASSCHENDAELE. 3 Coys in the front line and 1 in support, 33rd Div. on	
			the right, 7th R.B. on the left. The relief and the whole tour were most unpleasant owing to heavy shell fire. A number	
			of the HQ officers and men suffered from some form of gas poisoning though it was not known how they got it, and the symptoms	
			only developed after relief. a/Capt. D. Allhusen and 2/Lieut D. Mackenzie (latter 8th London Regt. attached) were wounded and the casualties	
			among O.R. were Killed 16. Wounded 33. Wounded and Missing 1.	MJSA
BRANDHOEK	8th		Bn. was relieved night 8th/9th by 6th KOYLI and moved to Brandhoek in Divisional Reserve, and on the 19th to Junction Camp in	
JUNCTION CAMP	19th		Divisional Support.	MJSA
			The following officers left the Battalion. Invalided to England 2/Lieut F.L. Trotter 27.11.17, Captain & Adjt. H.A. Jackson and Lieut	
			J.E.M. Macgregor 19.12.17. Captain R.C. Procter & 2/Lieut F.H. Newman ^ & 2/Lieut S.R. Wheston went to F.A. 2/Lieut S. Hodson cross posted to	
			9th Bn 20.12.17.	MJSA
			The following officers joined or re-joined. 2/Lieuts T.G. Graham, H.J. Rathbone, J. Macdonald (from 9th Bn) and H.S. Cook.	
Trenches	22nd		On the night 22nd/23rd Bn. took over the line N. of Passchendaele in Sheet 28 V 30 from the 5th Oxf. and Bucks L.I.	
			3 Coys in front line and 1 in reserve, 7th R.B. on the right 8th KRR. on the left. The Bn. only went in 230 strong,	

A6945 Wt. W11422/M1160 350,000 12/16 D. D. & L. Forms/C./2118/14.

Instructions regarding War Diaries and Intelligence Summaries are contained in F. S. Regs., Part II. and the Staff Manual respectively. Title pages will be prepared in manuscript.

WAR DIARY

~~or~~

~~INTELLIGENCE SUMMARY.~~

(Erase heading not required.)

Army Form C. 2118.

Place	Date	Hour	Summary of Events and Information	Remarks and references to Appendices
			[illegible]	
			[illegible]	
			[illegible]	
WIELTJE	26th		[illegible]	
			[illegible]	
			[illegible]	
LEULINE	27th		[illegible]	
			[illegible]	
			[illegible]	[illegible]
			[illegible]	
			[illegible]	
			[illegible]	
			[illegible] Major	

7th (S) Bn. K. R. R. Corps.

The average strength of Battalion during the month of December 1917 was 39 Officers 667 Other Ranks.

During the month :-

Off	O.R.	
6.	69	were admitted to F.A.
2.	24	" Evac. out of the Divl. area
1	22	rejoined from F.A.
3	23	of those admitted during December remain in F.A.

31st December 1917. M J St Aubyn Major

Comdg. 7th (S) Bn. K. R. R. C.

Secret

WO 95/1876 ?

9th (Service) Battalion

The King's Royal Rifle Corps

War Diary

From 1st to 31st January 1918

Volume 33.

4th (S) Bn. K R Rifles.

Instructions regarding War Diaries and Intelligence Summaries are contained in F. S. Regs., Part II. and the Staff Manual respectively. Title pages will be prepared in manuscript.

WAR DIARY for JANUARY 1918

or ~~INTELLIGENCE SUMMARY.~~

(Erase heading not required.)

Army Form C. 2118.

VOLUME 33

Place	Date	Hour	Summary of Events and Information	Remarks and references to Appendices
LEULINE	31.XII 1917		On this date 2Lt F.H. NEWMAN attached from the 8th London Regt, went to England sick	JB
"	2.1.18		The Bn left the LEULINE area, marching to St OMER and entraining there about 10 pm. 2Lt F. EVANS evacuated sick. Detrained at EDGEHILL on the 3rd and marched from there to VAUX SUR SOMME, into rest billets.	JB
VAUX-SUR-SOMME	3—22.1.18		Three weeks of training, during very cold weather. The Bn won the Divisional Army Rifle Association Competition by a broad margin, the successful platoon being No 3 under 2Lt J. KETCHELL. A Divisional Football Competition was held, in the 1st round of which the Bn defeated the 8th Rifle Brig, but lost in the end to the 8th K.R.R.C. Training was chiefly confined to Lewis Gun and Bombing classes	JB
	6.1.18		Captain R.C. PROCTER, attached from the 2/17th London Regt to England sick.	
	9.1.18		2Lt S.C. WAISTON to England sick.	
			On the 22nd the Bn began to move South, marching on successive days to VILLERS AUX-ERABLES, ROYE, JUSSY, CLASTRES. The average distance per day was 17 miles, and the roads very bad, but the Bn marched well. On the 26th the Brigade relieved the French in the line S. of St QUENTIN, the Bn being in support at CLASTRES. On the 29th C and D Coys moved up to ESSIGNY, and on the 30th B Coy moved to LA SABLIERE FARM, outside ESSIGNY.	JB
	24.1.18		Capt. H.A. JACKSON rejoined Bn from England.	
	27.1.18		Capt T.A. WATSON, M.C., RAMC, att ceased to be attached to the Bn, being relieved by Lt H.A. FEATHERSTONE, RAMC	
	26.1.18		2Lt F. EVANS rejoined Bn from Field Ambulance.	J Burch Lt Col. Cmdg. 7 K.R.R.C.

A6945 Wt. W11422/M1160 350,000 12/16 D. D. & L. Forms/C./2118/14.

7th (S) Bn. Kings Royal Rifle Corps.

The average strength of Battalion during the month of January 1918 was 37 Officers 762 Other Ranks

Of the above:-

O.	O.R.	
1	21	were admitted to F.A.
	10	were Evacuated out of the Divl. area
1	8	rejoined from F.A.
	3	Still remain in F.A.

J.S. Birch

Lieut.-Col.

Comd. 7th (S) Bn.
Kings Royal Rifles

31st January 1918.

7th (S) Bn King's Royal Rifle Corps

Alterations to rolls of men proceeding with Bn

Regtl No	Rank	Name		No of Sheet	Remarks
R11970	Rfn	Carr	F	4	To Base Depot 20/12
R10984	"	Thorpe	R	7	Evac Div Area 20/12
R12660	"	Parrock	W	8	"
R6248	"	Austin	J	9	" " " "
R11985	"	Bridges	W	10	To Base Depot 20/12
R12677	"	Buckley	J	10	Evac. Div Area 20/12
A3101	"	Foy	W	10	" " " "
R9581	"	Jacomb		11	" " " "
R11606	"	Johnson		11	" " " "
R13176	"	King		11	" " " "
R11969	"	Mitchell		11	" " " "
R12120	"	O'Mara		11	To Base Depot 20/12
R11216	"	Pound		12	Evac. Div Area 20/12
R12550	"	Smith		12	To Base Depot 20/12
R6374	Sgt.	Thompson		14	Evac Div Area 20/12
R10211	Rfn	Freeman		17	To Base Depot 20/12
R11174	"	Pickett		19	Evac. Div. Area 20/12
A477	"	Taylor		20	" " " "
A478	Cpl	Mead		22	" " " "
R9864	Rfn	Brooks		23	To Base Depot 20/12
A1406	"	Ralph		26	" " " "

J Bromwald Capt
for Lt Col
Comdg 7th KRR

[illegible]	[illegible]	A.C.	
[illegible]	[illegible]	C.C.	
[illegible]	[illegible]	T.P.	
	[illegible]	A.C.	
	[illegible]	M.C.	
	[illegible]	[illegible]	
	[illegible]	[illegible]	
	~~[illegible]~~	~~[illegible]~~	
	[illegible]	[illegible]	
	[illegible]	[illegible]	
	[illegible]	C.	
	[illegible]	A.C.	
	[illegible]	[illegible]	
	Mc[illegible]	[illegible]	
[illegible]	L. [illegible]	M.S.	[illegible]
[illegible]	[illegible]	G.	[illegible]
[illegible]	Mc[illegible]	G.	F.A.M.C

"A" Co. 7th K.R. Rifles

Regt. No.	Rank & Name			Remarks.
6330	C.S.M.	Hebblethwaite	E.	
6547	C.Q.M.	Coley	H.	
A 1	C.S.M.	Garnham	G.	
A 509	Sgt.	Ellis	S.	
A 15		Presslee	J.	
A 40		Downing	E.	
A 621		Chambers	F.	
A 2158		Plant	J.	
6/4570		Margiman	G.	
A 176	L/Sgt.	Mott	E.	
A 405	Cpl.	Wright	[illegible]	
7422		Church	J.	
R 11769		Hardy	W.	
A 87		Eaton	F.	
A 3097		Whitney	H.	
A 2009		Deakin	W.	
R 2017		Beck	G.	
R 11354		Stanford	E.	
A 28	L/C.	Smith	W.	
R 2092		Howarth	E.	
A 111		Hatton	T.	
A 1608		Atkins	R.	
A 91		Elliott	W.	
A 3365		Dunn	J.	
A 3369		Graham	J.	
A 861		Poulton	J.	
598		Plush	W.E.	
R 12085		Eaton	J.	
A 724		Blackman	E.	
A 696		Bradstreet	H.	
A 245		Moody	W.	
A 3357		Kimberly	J.	
[illegible]		[illegible]	[illegible]	

2

A Company 9th K.R.R.C.

Regtl No.	Rank & Name			Remarks
~~Rugby~~	~~Pte~~	~~Baswell~~	~~G.~~	
A 590	.	Brown	T.	
Y/1502	.	Barton	T.	
A 246	.	Brown	E.	
A 83	.	Bicknell	C.	
A 8338	.	Butler	H.	
~~R [illegible]~~		~~Blewitt~~	~~J.~~	
R 11213	.	Ball	F.	
8732	.	Brown	A.	
10453	.	Baldwin	D.	
R 661	.	Cotterill	J.	
A 17	.	Condict	F.	
A 3781	.	Cutten	S.	
A 699	.	Coker	G.H.	
R 10382	.	Collis	C.	
A 86	.	Carroll	A.	
R 7412	.	Crowder	C.	
11994	.	Chittell	J.	
1296	.	Cassidy	F.	
R 11975	.	Cheetham	S.	
R 11878	.	Cooper	W.	
Y 788		Cooper	G.	
12243	.	Card	T.	
~~R 11995~~	.	~~Crompton~~	~~A.~~	
R 11716	.	Cocker	J.	
A 63	.	Curley	E.	
11970		Carr	F.	
A 3083	.	Donald	B.	
R 11188		Davies	A.	
R 8324		Denny	C.	
R 8834	.	Dickens	E.	

A Company 7th [illegible]

Regt. No.	Rank	Name		Remarks
1205	Pte	Harris	J.	
13288	.	Holden	T.	
A 2948	.	Jones	E.	
R 5115	.	Insley	J.	
R 11073	.	Johnson	W.	
~~[illegible]~~		~~[illegible]~~	~~J.~~	
A 5	.	Ingram	T.	
R 5425	.	Jobey	S.	
A 222	.	Johnson	W.	
A 3446	.	Kingham	A.	
A 191	.	Kipling	J.	
A 2791	.	Kitchener	G.	
1208	.	Keep	H.	
5542	.	Kenward	S.	
A 3079	.	Ledbrook	W.	
A 3421	.	Lake	C.	
R 2082	.	Lambert	E.	
R 5421	.	Lee	B.G.	
R 6040	.	Lemere	J.	
R 8008	.	Milward	J.	
A 323	.	Mayling	H.	
11279	.	Malham	E.	
A 403	.	Martin	R.	
A 488	.	Matthews	W.	
R 11850	.	Maggs	E.	
6/1378	.	McDonnell	H.	
1312	.	Middleton	G.	
1909	.	McDonald	W.	
20469	.	Martin	C.	

"A" Company 7th K.R.R.C.

Regtl. No.	Rank	Name		Remarks
R 1152	Rfn	Walker	R.	
R 2102	.	Wallis	R.	
A 485	.	Ward	J.	
A 65	.	White	G.	
R 7188	.	Wilde	E.	
A 6	.	Wilson	H.	
R 3290	.	Wood	A	
A 169	.	Woods	F.	
R 1395	.	Walls	R	
A 117	.	Williams	R	
R 76	.	Wilson	A	
12495	.	Wren	J.	
A 2205	.	Wadman	C.	
2209	.	Yates	F	
Y 1103	.	Kitcher	H	W. Ramsay 2/Lt
Y 326	A/Cpl	Longley	R	for O.C.
R 2772	Rfn	McCarthy		"A" Coy.
R 12660	.	Parrock	W	7th K.R.R.C.
1312	.	Middleton		
R 8007	.	Smith	J	
Y 1667	.	Thornley	L	
6/1177	.	Woodhall	J	
Y 326	.	Foyle		
R 8333		Hayes	F	
4172	Sgt	Jenkinson	F	

B

7th K R R

Nominal Roll Continued

No	Rank & Name			Remarks
Y 1514	Rfn	Burcham	W	
Y 1213	"	Burcham	R	
A 605	"	Burstowe	H	
R 11964	"	Bridges	W	
2077	"	Brooks	A	
A 3441	"	Brown	W	
R 12620	"	Brown	F	
R 9457	"	Brown	D	
1690	"	Bunn	W	
R 12677	"	Buckley	F	
A 479	"	Burrows	A	
R 3526	"	Burley	A	
A 606	"	Bygham	W	
A 703	"	Champion	W	
A 556	"	Channon	W	
4920	"	Child	F	
R 10815	"	Chopping	F	
R 10539	"	Chopping	W	
R 9771	"	Caddle	W	
A 1275	"	Collins	T	
R 6205	"	Coote	W	
A 508	"	Cornell	F	
A 3647	"	Cooper	J	
R 11876	"	Cobbler	K	
A 753	"	Coates	E	
R 10623	"	Cox	S	
R 8202	"	Cutcher	T	
A 1759	"	Cobb	A	
R 11119	"	Coventry	L	
[illegible]	"	Crewther	J	
A 557	"	Darby	W	
A 5046	"	Dempster	B	
R 10356	"	Duffield	W	
A 1896	"	Dobson	A	
A 551	"	Eagles	H	
R 6308	"	Eccleston	H	
A 514	"	Essele	S	
R 6521	"	Faghun	J	
A 198	"	Fahey	J	
Y 428	"	Fieldhouse	J	
R 11857	"	Frisby	R	
A 3101	"	Fry	W	
R 9582	"	Fuller	G	
Y 1405	"	Fox	H	
R 6266	"	Giles	C	
R 9909	"	Gillman	G	
R 1323	"	Grimes	M	
R 2934	"	Greenfield	E	
R 11166	"	Hall	F	
11509	"	Harris	W	

10

[illegible]	[illegible]	[illegible]
[illegible]	[illegible]	[illegible]
[illegible]	[illegible]	[illegible]
[illegible]	[illegible]	[illegible]
[illegible]	[illegible]	[illegible]
[illegible]	Jordan	H
A 117	Jewell	[illegible]
[illegible]	Howell	B
[illegible]	Kent	A
[illegible]	[illegible]	F
[illegible]	[illegible]	W
[illegible]	Jackson	T
[illegible]	Jones	G
[illegible]	Jones	G
[illegible]	[illegible]	W
[illegible]	Johnson	J
[illegible]	Johnson	H
[illegible]	[illegible]	W
[illegible]	[illegible]	T
[illegible]	King	F
A 1317	Kelly	A
A 11674	King	H
A 11607	Kitchen	T
A 11731	Lee	H
A 7160	Leach	W
A 8022	Lemmon	T
A 11239	Jeffard	A
A 770	[illegible]	A
A 10055	[illegible]	J
A 11157	Madden	U
A 11511	Martin	T
A 10573	Martin	F
A 11110	Mackay	C
A 1227	[illegible]	B
A 1535	Mager	B
A 1452	[illegible]	J
A 1962	[illegible]	G
A 1501	MacThomas	G
A 1119	McFarlane	F
A 1412	Meer	B
A 1465	Mitchell	A
A 545	Morley	F
A 1271	Moore	D
A 906	Moore	A
A 3512	Young	F
A 1708	[illegible]	F
A 11534	[illegible]	F
A 171	[illegible]	H
A 172	[illegible]	F
9495	[illegible]	C
A 12120	O'[illegible]	J
A 6328	Ogden	F
A 3266	Palmer	A

11

54

B Coy 7th K.R.R.

Nominal Roll Continued

No	Rank & Name			Remarks
R 11819	Rfn	Parkinson	J	
R 12132	"	Patching	E	
R 6939	"	Perks	H	
A 3091	"	Peatfield	T	
R 11415	"	Pembleton	J	
R 11351	"	Pidcock	R	
A 397	"	Pickthall	D	
R 8411	"	Pickholtze	M	
R 9964	"	Porter	H	
11216	"	Pound	H	
R 11460	"	Pratt	W	
R 13060	"	Quartley	H	
A 2949	"	Randall	J	
A 895	"	Rea	T	
A 745	"	Richardson	G	
A 2370	"	Richardson	J	
R 6641	"	Renvoize	F	
R 6667	"	Rudkin	J	
R 11720	"	Samples	J	
A 350	"	Scrivens	C	
A 474	"	Schofield	F	
A 491	"	Sinclair	J	
R 6288	"	Smith	V	
R 10738	"	Smith	H	
R 11446	"	Smith	J	
R 12050	"	Smith	J	
A 3157	"	Smith	H	
2073	"	Smith	E	
V 260	"	Smith	J	
R 6340	"	Smith	R	
R 11901	"	Styles	R	
R 11279	"	Slater	W.	
R 8295	"	Stones	G	
R 10699	"	Sweeney	P	
V 538	"	Taylor	A	
R 9213	"	Thompson	A	
R 12670	"	Thorpe	B	
R 1707	"	Tipton	H	
R 13120	"	Turner	J	
B 49	"	Telford	K	
R 11469	"	Tickell	W	
R 13227	"	Tilbin	J	
A 3098	"	Vizarage	M	
R 10773	"	Wade	W	
A 3163	"	Waterhouse	J	
R 2873	"	Walters	F	
R 6332	"	Weston	P	
R 7184	"	Wensley	H	
A 472	"	Wheeler	H.	
~~R 12100~~		~~Whitehead~~	~~H~~	
R 11413	"	Whitehead	M.	
A 956	"	Whitehouse	J	
R 11311	"	White	H	
R 7053	"	Whittaker	G	

12

54

Nominal Roll Continued

No	Rank & Name		Remarks
A 1265	Rfn	Wenham C	
A 1112	"	Whitby J	
V 266	"	W[illegible] E	
V 152	"	Wise E	
R 11765	"	Wynn W	
A 1165	"	Young A	
[illegible] 4774	"	Jennings H	

14/12/15

[illegible] Lieut.

Comdg B Coy

7th K R R

1st Coy. 7th H.R.R.C.

Reg. No.	Rank	Name		Remarks
a 1158	S.M.	Paul,	C.	
5921	C.S.M.	Stanston,	A.	
1535	C/Sgt.	Bardick,	J.	
G 813	Sgt.	Acres,	J.	
9473	"	Rayne,	F.	
a 215	"	Foster,	B.	
a 659	"	Robbins,	C.	
R 3037	"	Tabberer,	H.R.	
1307	"	Thompson,		
a 1062	"	Towndey,	C.	
6362	"	Wilson,	J.	
R 6534	A/Sgt.	Shepherd,	L.	
Y 1725	Cpl.	Atkins,	J.	
10603	"	Bunting,	W.	
3210	"	Edwards,	W.	
R 5	"	Mercy,	C.	
Y 1728	"	Morgan,	A	
a 1570	"	Oldham,	A	
R 10	"	Rogers,	J.	
Y 1839	"	Wood,	C	
R 5672	L/Cpl.	Bailey,	C.	
R 3038	"	Brunton,	T.	
R 6452	"	Brain,	E. F.	
R 116	"	Foster,	C.	
~~R 1522~~	~~"~~	~~Fotheringham,~~	~~L.~~	
R 522	"	Hall,	W.	
2764	"	Kibble,	F.	
a 163	"	Poole,	B.	
7901	"	Silver,	F.	

14

15

3 C. Coy. of 4th K.R.R.C.

Reg. No.	Rank	Name	Remarks
R 340	Rfm	Butler, C.	
10417	"	Buxton, W.	
C 11347	"	Bramley, C.	
R 1262	"	Burdess, A.	
1191	"	Bucknell, A.	
9956	"	Collins, A.	
R 1441	"	Cuttle, J.	
R 1350	"	Crossland, H.	
7449	"	Comber, C.	
7331	"	Craft, C.	
A 3256	"	Cullen, D.	
~~R 11597~~	~~"~~	~~Durrant, G.~~	
A 3518	"	Darby, J.	
A 3552	"	Davies, W.	
801	"	Davies, B.	
1095	"	Daws, G.	
R 9126	"	Daws, F.	
~~R 10.61~~	~~"~~	~~Dowden, G.~~	
R 14	"	Dunn, F.	
		Derbyshire, F.	
R 7994	"	De Percy, H.	
R 1541	"	Dring, H.	
A 1352	"	Ebbage, A.	
A 712	"	Evans, J.	
R 126	"	Evans, H.	
A 2052	"	Ford, C.	
R 11495		Farrell, J.	
R 6258	"	Fitzgerald, C.	
R 9644	"	Flood, C.	

16

5th Coy 7th A. R. R. C.

Reg. No.	Rank	Name	Remarks
R 10381	Pte	Hewitt, E.	
a 1327	"	Hewitt, G.	
9909	"	Johnson, F.	
b 1117	"	James, W.	
a 3576	"	Jephcott, J.	
R 11333	"	Jackson, G.	
R 99144	"	John, S.	
R 11692	"	James, E.	
R 370	"	Kidder, F.	
R 1322	"	Knightly, W.	
1257	"	Kelly, J.	
R 10330	"	Kennedy, W.	
a 1255	"	Knight, R.	
R 11864	"	Kay, J.	
R 13209	"	Kelly, C.	
R 3665	"	Kenny, B.	
R 13150	"	Kerridge, E.	
1530	"	Livingston, W.	
1187	"	Lambert, R.	
R 11819	"	Larkin, J.	
R 3077	"	Lane, H.	
R 13051	"	Lord, J.	
R 13071	"	Lightfoot, W.	
R 13151	"	Lideman, J.	
R 11560	"	Macon, F.	
R 10887	"	McCarthy, J.	
R 1627	"	McIntosh, R.	
a 1359	"	Mahoney, J.	

18

~~24~~

L. C. Corp. 7th K. R. R. C.

Reg. No.	Rank	Name	Remarks
1102	Rfn	[illegible] H.	
560	"	Radford, W.	
[illegible]	"	Richardson, G.	
900	"	Richardson, G.	
[illegible]	"	[illegible]	
~~[illegible]~~		~~[illegible]~~	
[illegible]	"	[illegible] G.	
[illegible]9	"	Shaw W.	
201	"	Skinner, H.	
1135	"	Smith. W.	
134	"	Smith. W.	
1060	"	Smith. G.	
11140	"	[illegible] H.	
852	"	Slater. J.	
1101	"	Scott. G.	
960	"	Smith. H.	
1195	"	Somers. H.	
10663	"	Skillicorn, W.	
1053	"	Sutton, H.	
11695	"	Sparrow. H.	
11544	"	Stimson, J.	
1204	"	Thompson, G.	
1800	"	Tomlinson, W	
1177	"	Taylor. L.	
513	"	Taylor. H.	
233	"	Taylor. H.	
2663	"	[illegible] H.	
11507	"	Till. C.	
2903	"	Tuthill, G.	
1066	"	Walker, J.	
351	"	Withers. A.	
10026	"	Windibank. J.	
11449	"	Walton, R.	

20

[illegible]

[illegible]		[illegible]
[illegible]		[illegible]
[illegible]		[illegible]
[illegible]		[illegible]
[illegible]		[illegible]
[illegible]		[illegible]
[illegible]		[illegible]
[illegible]		[illegible]
[illegible]		[illegible]
[illegible]		Wright, J.
[illegible]		[illegible]
[illegible]		[illegible]
[illegible]		Young, J.
[illegible]		[illegible]

21

D Coy 7th K.R. Rfs

Regt No	Rank & Name		Remarks
1551	CSM	Jones	
A93	CQMS	Scriggs E.	
5904	Sergt	Dickinson S.	
7964	"	Benbow W.	
9555	"	Jones A.	
A1466	"	Bailey W.	
8545	"	Pullow P.	
A2445	"	Austin H	
R6646	A/Sergt	Marshall W.	
A3274	"	Dakson H.	
5707	Cpl.	Southey F.	
R7575	"	Cooper H	
A1354	"	Lewis A.	
A1529	"	Hutchinson W.	
A3449	"	Ward G.	
A2346	"	Meredith F.	
A1277	a/Cpl	Osborne E.	
A475	Cpl	Mead H ~~[illegible]~~ /17	Sick in Hpl.
R[illegible]	a/Cpl.	Clarke F.	
7475	"	Marlow W.	
R10619	L/Cpl	Swales J.	
A1577	"	Berry W.	
R6582	"	Forrest W. H	
R6592	"	Bailey J.W.	
R6422	"	Clegg J.	
R7954	"	O'Riley F.	
A2938	"	Harrison F.	
R6675	"	Halton J.	
R6315	"	Kent E.	
A1750	"	Wells W.	
A1719	"	Heaver H	
A1718	"	Marsh H.	
R1606	"	Potter A.	
R717	"	Redfern A.	
71574	"	Lewis J.	
R6418	"	Bray R.	

22

36

No.	Rank	Name	Remarks
R[illegible]361	Pte	Cole A.	
R6575		[illegible]	
R1371		[illegible]	
R[illegible]		[illegible]	
[illegible]		[illegible]	
10573		Campbell G.	
R11245	Do	Ashworth J.	
R7574		Adams J.	
R10949		Ash F.	
R[illegible]		Ashbourne H.	[illegible]
R9535		Allen J.	[illegible]
R6591		Acton W.	[illegible]
R5472		[illegible] F.	[illegible]
R5010		Bradley J.	
R16411		Bosworth S.	
R6400		Ball J.	[illegible]
R2944		Bowers E.	
R11377		Burns J.	
R[illegible]		Barnes H.	
R[illegible]		Burbank W.	
R[illegible]		Burrell A.	
R[illegible]		Baker B.	
R[illegible]		Brown J.	
R1136		Barton G.	
R7424		Boyle J.	
R1921		Bell E.	
R1778		Baker T.	
R13290		Boon H.	
R2733		Beach G.	
R7055		Brown G.	
R11425		Burke J.	
R9564		Brooks H.	
R[illegible]		[illegible] G.	
R1631		[illegible]	
R6555		Chaddaway J.	
12055		Crawford J.	
R[illegible]		Clegg H.	
R[illegible]		Cobb G.	
12092		Chapman A.	
R[illegible]		[illegible] S.	
[illegible]		[illegible]	

D Coy 7th K R Rifles

Regl No.	Rank & Name		Remarks
R11914	Rfn.	Cain W.	
R6661	"	Crosbie G.	Sick in Hpl
R6650	"	Dunthwaite J.	
R6425	"	Dickenson J.	
R6659	"	Dickenson J.	
A1579	"	Dyde J.	
A2347	"	Darlow W.	
R6318	"	Edmonds T.	
R10571	"	Evans H.	
R6699	"	Ellis J.	
5092	"	Evans G.	
R17909	"	Eale R.	Sick in Hpl
A1405	"	French W.	
R11549	"	Foreman R.	
R6543	"	Fawcett A.	
R6675	"	Fullerton W.	
R6679	"	Firth J.	
A3271	"	Good W.	
A1651	"	Griffiths T.	
A1358	"	Grange H.	
R6726	"	Gray H.	
R11971	"	George J.	
11973	"	Gardner G.	Sick in Hpl
A1538	"	Hannan W.	
A1426	"	Heath E.	
A1364	"	Hill E.	
A1409	"	Hand A.	
R6705	"	Harris J.	
R4770	"	Horner J.	
R11929	"	Haggar H.	
A593	"	Holmes J.	
7356	"	Hesslewood W.	
A3652	"	Haigh J.	
R6671	"	Harrist H.	
71503	"	Howe J.	
R6878	"	Hewlett W.	Sick in Hpl
~~R6706~~	~~"~~	~~Hartley W.~~	Sick in Hpl
R77	"	Hadfield J.	Road Board
A1360	"	Johnson E.	
R6718	"	Jennings J.	
A2943	"	Johnson W.	
R10308	"	Jackson J.	
R2195	"	Kemp H.	
A1367	"	Kirby W.	
R6716	"	Kemp J.	
R6662	"	Kenton A.	

J 4

R5939	Pte	[illegible] J
R12153		Firth J
R1121		[illegible] J
R7710		Ford A
R11630		Fox J
S2495		Fox E
R1295		[illegible] A
R6544		Vaughan J
R5281		[illegible] C
R6555		[illegible] J
R11222		[illegible] J
R6310		Meyer E
R2571		Mills A
R2563		Millichip J
R11455		Mee J
R6925		Marshall G.
R14903		Marshall H
R11665		McCarthy C T
R12939		Marsh W
R12129		May A.
R5203		Murphy W.
R2937		Millward H
R11537		Mason E
R11496		[illegible] J
R12544		Miller G
G1211		Mills W.
R2996		Morrow P
R1252		[illegible] J
R11151		Neal C
R11445		Nottingham C
R1146		Nicholls J
R6835		O'Connell J
R11733		Oakes J
R1869		Pointing H
R5024		[illegible] S
G1338		[illegible] J
R1579		Parker A
R13188		Poynton J
R1981		[illegible] A
R2565		Pope J
R10983		Parkins G
R15031		Phillips A

25

D Coy 9th R R Rifles

Regt No	Rank & Name		Remarks
A806	Rfn	Payton C.	
R12497	"	Peake W.	
R10669	"	Phipps J.	
R12936	"	Parker E.	
R10057	"	Pearce W.	
R11451	"	Pearce C.	
A1406	"	Ralph J.	
A1147	"	Roberts J.	
A2551	"	Rudge W.	
R1648	"	Ready E.	
A1850	"	Robinson A	
R6539	"	Reeve E.	
R12194	"	Rodgers J.	
R7949	"	Robinson M.	
A1307	"	Symonds A.	
R1646	"	Steadman J.	
A1527	"	Stafford A.	
R6538	"	Simpson A.W.	
R11624	"	Stoneley S.	
R11726	"	Stafford W.	
R13165	"	Schofield H	
R12577	"	Sheppherd J	
R13156	"	Smith A	
R6559	"	Slade F	
R13057	"	Steer W.	
~~R11030~~		~~Smith A.~~	
A1454	"	Swaine J.	
A1765	"	Thomas D.	
A1359	"	Thompson L.	
R7376	"	Tibbetts H.	
R6697	"	Tipping H.	
R9357	"	Tyers D.	
R10836	"	Tomlinson W.	
R12160	"	Tonge H.	
A1465	"	Upton W.	
A3655	"	Varnish A	
R6690	"	Venning L.	
10381	"	Walbourne E	
A1427	"	Webb H.	
R2103	"	Wood H.	
R1519	"	Ward J	
R8471	"	Wright G	
R6677	"	Wilson J	
R6544	"	Williams D.	
R8422	"	Wilkinson J.	26
R11524	"	Wylde F.	
Y1510	"	Dickens J	

www.ingramcontent.com/pod-product-compliance
Lightning Source LLC
Chambersburg PA
CBHW082007220426
43670CB00014B/2575

* 9 7 8 1 4 7 4 5 0 8 9 4 0 *